Pony Express

Pony Express

FRED REINFELD

UNIVERSITY OF NEBRASKA PRESS   LINCOLN

Library of Congress Catalog Card Number: 64–21330

International Standard Book Number 0–8032–5786–4

First Bison Book printing: October 1973

Most recent printing shown by first digit below:
1   2   3   4   5   6   7   8   9   10

Bison Book edition reproduced from the first (1966) edition by arrangement with the Publisher.

Manufactured in the United States of America

Contents

Pony Express

1 *"California, Here I Come!"*

"WANTED—young, skinny, wiry fellows, not over 18. Must be expert riders, willing to risk death daily. Orphans preferred. Wages $25 a week. . . ."

When this notice appeared in a San Francisco paper in 1860, half a million Americans lived west of the Rocky Mountains—300,000 in California. Two thousand miles of mountains, plains, and deserts, broken only by Indian trails, separated them from the rest of the United States. To link California to the Missouri frontier, an adventurous businessman created the Pony Express.

Like the covered-wagon pioneers, the Pony Express riders suffered from heat and thirst in the desert; in the wintertime they found the mountain passes virtually blockaded by deep piles of snow; on the plains furious blizzards made traveling hazardous. Added to these dangers was the ever present threat of Indian attack.

Though the Pony Express lasted for only eighteen months, it occupies a glorious place in American history. To this day, the Pony Express remains a symbol of swift service, the spirit of adventure and faithful execution of a very exacting and dangerous task. For sheer heroic endurance, it probably does not have its equal in American history.

It all started, in a sense, on that day in 1839, when a Swiss adventurer named John Sutter arrived in Monterey in Upper California, then under Mexican rule. By taking Mexican citizenship Sutter prevailed on Alvarado, the Mexican governor, to grant him a large tract of land near the present San Francisco.

Wedded as he was to the easygoing ways of the Spaniards and Mexicans, Alvarado viewed the arrival of any foreigner with suspicion and distrust. But Sutter cleverly overcame the governor's reluctance.

Nearby, he pointed out to the governor, was a fortified Russian fur-trading post on Bodega Bay. The fur, trade had seen its most profitable days and the Russians were ready to pull out in any event.

Sutter made arrangements to acquire the fort from the Russians. Now, he explained to Alvarado, he could garrison the fort and thus keep Indians and outlaws in check. Convinced by this argument, the governor presented Sutter with a magnificent tract of land at the confluence of the American and Sacramento rivers.

So the fort became Fort Sutter, and Sutter built himself a fine house, barracks for his men, and a storage house for the products raised on his thousands of acres. Around these buildings he put up a wall of redwood logs.

In time, to the discomfort of the uneasy Mexicans, Sutter's fort became the headquarters of Americans coming to California. The "mountain men," those intrepid trappers of the west, made Fort Sutter their rendezvous, as did the exploring parties of adventurous Americans who were attracted by the promise of California's lush land and flourishing herds.

So extensive became Sutter's little "empire" that by 1848, it contained about a quarter of the handful of Americans then living in California.

The Mexicans feared and hated these newcomers.

Now that Texas had achieved its independence from Mexican rule, might not the same thing happen in California? Sometimes the worried Mexican officials drove out American newcomers; sometimes they imprisoned them and held them for heavy ransom.

When war broke out between the United States and Mexico in 1846, General John C. Fremont was conducting a scientific expedition in Upper California, and a small squadron under Commander John D. Sloat happened to be cruising off the California coast. Sloat landed marines at Monterey, raised the American flag there and then proceeded to capture Fort Yerba Buena (later to become San Francisco).

As for Fremont, he put himself at the head of a small American force, unfurled the Bear Flag and captured Sonoma and General Vallejo, the Mexican commander. Later on, Fremont was court-martialed on the charge of having acted without orders. But no matter—California had become American soil.

After the Mexican War was over, quite a few returned veterans found work with John Sutter. He needed all the help he could get, for he was building a flour mill near his fort and a sawmill on the American River.

Life at Sutter's fort was pleasant and tranquil until that fateful day in February, 1848, when James Marshall, who was in charge of constructing the sawmill, discovered gold on Sutter's property. This was how Sutter later described his first reaction to Marshall's excited arrival:

I was sitting one afternoon, just after my siesta, engaged, bye the bye, in writing a letter to a relation of mine in Lucerne, when I was interrupted by Mr. Marshall, a gentleman with whom I had frequent business transactions—bursting hurriedly into the room. From the unusual agitation in his manner I imagined something serious had occurred, and, as we involuntarily do in this part of the world, I glanced to see if my rifle was in its proper place.

When Marshall blurted out the story of his sensational find, Sutter was skeptical. But when Marshall showed him some of the gold flakes, Sutter was convinced. The next day they went down to the millrace in the river, and there found many more traces of gold.

Their decision to keep secret the discovery of the gold proved futile. "As soon as we came back to the mill," Sutter later recalled, "we noticed by the excitement of the working people that we had been dogged about, and to complete our disappointment, one of the Indians who had worked at the gold mine in the neighborhood of La Paz, cried out in showing us some specimens picked up by himself, 'Oro! Oro! Oro!' "

So that was the end of the secret. As soon as the news spread over San Francisco the gold rush was on. Workers downed their tools; sailors deserted their ships; farmers left their fields in the middle of plowing. Even many of John Sutter's employees gave up their jobs to pan for gold in the sand-and-gravel bed of the American River.

As fast as whaling ships put in at the San Francisco Bay, their seamen deserted. This happened with no fewer than sixteen vessels. Wages shot up madly. Whereas whaling seamen had been paid about two dollars a month, they now began to receive one hundred and fifty dollars a month. As for whaling captains, their pay multiplied by as much as ten times. Even so, a crewman from the whaler *Pacific* wrote his family that "our captain has concluded to go to the mines instead of proceeding on a whaling voyage. He intends to take all hands with him, and give us two-thirds of the gold we procure."

Gradually, the word spread back East that gold had been discovered in California. In reading about the California gold rush, we get the impression that the discovery of gold in February, 1848, immediately led to a mad stampede from the east. Actually this was not so. It was not until the following September that people began to perk up their ears.

Why the delay? It is difficult for us to realize how slowly the word traveled back. Much of this "news" was in the form of wild rumor that, on the face of it, seemed to make no sense. Then, consider the conditions under which news was carried. To bring word of the electrifying discovery across the mountains and deserts to Salt Lake City took many weeks. Months passed before the news was accepted in Missouri.

But when President Polk soberly mentioned the gold discoveries in his December, 1848, message to Congress, interest began to quicken. Later, the War Department put a box of gold fragments on public display. After this, interest really mushroomed.

Soon the country was seized by a veritable gold madness. Stories went the rounds that anyone could become rich in California by picking up gold from the ground or panning it in any stream. Everyone back east was in a frenzy to come to California and strike it rich.

Still, it was not until the summer of 1849, some sixteen months after the discovery of gold, that the Forty-Niners were to set out in their covered wagons to reach the promised land.

Meanwhile, it was winter and overland traveling was out of the question. The first pioneers to reach the gold fields came by ship. Some of them sailed, at exorbitant prices, in miserable unseaworthy vessels that should have been retired from service years earlier. Some men, those who had the means, formed a cooperative, raising enough money to buy a ship and have it properly repaired.

Passage often cost as much as a thousand dollars, a large sum in those days. Some people sold their homes or businesses at a sacrifice. Others pawned everything they owned. By January of the new year, a serious labor shortage developed in the east as men prepared to leave for California. At the same time, the kind of implements that would be needed in California—guns, pickaxes, shovels, and the like—likewise became scarce.

In those days, a voyage to California was not only expensive—it was also dangerous, tedious, and filled with hardship and anxiety from beginning to end. Cramped quarters, miserable food, seasickness, and unbearable boredom were the lot of every passenger.

The trip around Cape Horn, about fifteen thousand miles long, usually lasted some six months. A sailing ship sometimes took a month to round the Horn, buffeted by vicious storms and rolling seas. The route by way of Panama was shorter by several thousand miles, but the journey across the disease-infested jungle took a great toll in human life. Those who were lucky enough to come out of the jungle alive often found that no ship was available when they reached the Pacific side. In the

Forty-Niners sailed around Cape Horn to California in search of gold.

PONY EXPRESS HISTORY AND ART GALLERY

The steamer Antelope carried Pony Express mail from Sacramento
to San Francisco.

end, many of those who thought they would get a head start by sailing to California actually gained little or no time as against the pioneers who left much later to travel by land.

By early spring of 1849, the frontier towns of Missouri were filled with covered wagons. Business in these towns flourished as men left their jobs and professions to seek their fortunes in California. Most of the wagon trains took the Oregon Trail, turning south after they crossed the Rockies. Some used the Santa Fe Trail, traveling in a southerly direction and then turning north and west.

When a wagon train halted toward sundown, the wagons were arranged in a circle or square for protection against Indian raiders. At this time the danger of Indian attack was not very great. But there were other dangers. Fierce prairie storms and cloudbursts could cause havoc, swelling streams and rivers so that these became hard to ford.

By the time the Forty-Niners were ready to cross the Rockies, they had discarded a good deal of their expensive equipment and furniture in order to lessen the burden for their weary oxen. Once over the Rockies, they found themselves in the terrible deserts of Utah and Nevada. The sun poured down on them pitilessly, and they suffered from thirst. What little water could be found was often poisonous because of its alkali content. At this stage, wagons and animals were often abandoned.

Then came the crossing of the Sierra Nevada Mountains, and at last they were in the promised land. But most of them had no thought of settling permanently in California. They wanted to make a fortune and go back

East to their homes, their families and their friends. They wanted desperately to be in touch with the East, and yet they were separated by some two thousand miles from the nearest frontier. The depressing sense of isolation was one of the hardest things that a pioneer had to endure.

2 *By Ocean and Desert*

WHAT MADE LIFE in California even more lonely was the lack of proper mail delivery between the West Coast and the East Coast. There were two land routes to Missouri, both of them highly unsatisfactory. The remaining mail route—by ocean and across Panama—was a bit better, but it had many irritating features.

The Panama route took about six weeks for mail delivery. It was a disheartening experience to read a newspaper six weeks stale. Worst yet, the schedules of the Pacific Mail Steamship Line were so unreliable that there was no telling just when a mail delivery would be arriving.

For this reason a semaphore was placed on Telegraph Hill in San Francisco. The signal arms were raised on the arrival of a mail steamer into the harbor. Then the settlers would wait in line at the post office for hours for their mail—and, often as not, they would wind up not getting any.

San Francisco had become the unofficial capital for a hinterland of mining camps and tent villages which dotted the banks of rivers and their tributary streams. And, despite the absence of roads, the steep canyons and wooded hills had their share of miners. Here the pack mules which brought in supplies also delivered newspapers that were sometimes more than three months old.

As a steady stream of newcomers kept arriving, the

towns and camps sprang up so rapidly that the Post Office Department could not keep up with them. Tons of "dead-letter" mail were piling up in the San Francisco post office. Soon, enterprising people were undertaking to deliver this unclaimed mail to such outlying places as Murderer's Bar, Dead Man's Gulch, and Hog's Glory. (What picturesque stories there must have been to account for these names!) And this was how the "Jackass Express"—one man and a mule—got its start.

Alexander H. Todd, who came to California by sea in June, 1849, was one of that small number of perceptive pioneers who realized that in many cases it was possible to make more money from the miners than from mining gold. Having come to this conclusion, he swiftly switched from mining to running an express service. It took very little time to find out that miners in the remote camps were willing to pay him—and pay him well—to deliver their mail from the post office.

For this service Todd charged one dollar to register a miner's name, and in addition he was promised an ounce of gold dust for each letter or parcel he delivered. As an ounce was worth over fifteen dollars, Todd decided that he would soon become a rich man—and so he did.

Right at the start Todd had an extraordinary experience. After leaving the camps he dropped in at the town of Stockton, where several people gave him nondescript packages to deliver to a San Francisco firm. After Todd did so, he discovered to his amazement that the packages had contained $250,000 worth of gold— entrusted to a complete stranger! For placing the packages in an old butter keg which he shipped by riverboat to San Francisco, Todd was paid $12,500.

On his arrival in town, Todd had himself sworn in as a postal clerk for the U.S. government, picked up the mail addressed to his customers, and bought all the newspapers he could lay his hands on. He had no trouble selling the papers to the miners for eight dollars apiece. Soon Todd's spectacular example had many imitators, and they all flourished even though competition forced them to reduce prices to a more realistic level.

Alonzo Delano, one of these competitors, has an interesting description of an expressman's arrival with the mail in his *Penknife Sketches*:

> The Express has arrived! Every pick and shovel is dropped, every pan is laid aside, every rocker is stopped with its half-washed dirt, every claim is deserted, and they crowd around the store with eager inquiries, "Have you got a letter for me?"
>
> With what joy it is seized, and they care little whether they pay two or five dollars for it, they've got a letter. Or perhaps, as is often the case, the answer is "There's nothing for you," and with a "Damn the luck" and a heavy heart, they go sullenly back to work, unfitted by disappointment for social intercourse for the rest of the day.

Joaquin Miller, who was a Forty-Niner and later became a famous writer, left this equally absorbing account of the early mail deliveries in California:

> The Pony Express was a great feature in the gold mines of California long before anyone ever thought of putting it on the plains. Every creek, camp or

"city" had its Pony Express which ran to and from the nearest office. At Yreka we had the Humbug Creek Express, the Deadwood Camp Express, the Greenhorn, and so on.

The rider was always a bold, bright young fellow, who owned the line, horses and all, and had his "office" in some responsible store. He crowded an immense deal of personality into his work; would die in the saddle rather than delay ten minutes over the expected time. He was, of course, always a dashing rider, dressed gayly and blew a small bugle as he went up and down the creek at a plunging rate. "Three blasts, after the fashion of the London postman!" Whack and bang at the cabin door meant a letter for this or that "claim," as the rider dashed down the trail under the trees.

And then hats in the air! Hurrah, hurrah, hurrah! Whose is it—and which one of the half-dozen or dozen men at the long sluice-boxes is to hear from his wife, mother or waiting sweetheart? This one starts to get it—that one, then the other. They look at one another hastily, and then one of them—strangely enough nearly always the right one!—springs up the ladder. Away, over the boulders with a bound, with pay for the letter clutched in his fist! He grasps the letter, away bounds the spirited pony, another blast of the horn!

From these vivid reminiscences we can glean some idea of the loneliness of the Californians and their anxiety to have an efficient mail route established. And yet the difficulties were appalling.

By the time the decade of the 1850s had arrived, the

railroads and telegraph lines stretched from the eastern seaboard to Missouri. But between Missouri and California there lay some two thousand miles, with a small part of the area inhabited by the Indians whose friendliness was problematical. A few remote towns completed the bleak picture.

This area was made up of plains, mountains and deserts. With no railroad available, the only way to cross to California was by horseback, covered wagon or stagecoach.

Moving freight from the Midwest to the Coast was a costly business that called for bold enterprise, careful planning, and superb management. The leading company in the field was the firm of Russell, Majors & Waddell. To be successful, they had to be first-class businessmen.

There were trails, to be sure, but they could not be used throughout, and only an expert could avoid losing his way. Much of the desert areas were covered with alkali dust, so poisonous that even desert growths could not flourish. The trails themselves were broken by rivers that could not be crossed during the spring floodtides. The rugged mountain ranges were fatal barriers to those who did not know the passes.

In the summer, the burning sun on prairie and desert was hard to bear. In winter, incessant snow piled up incredibly high drifts that brought many an unfortunate victim to a cruel end. But natural hardships were not the only dangers. Even when peace prevailed with one Indian tribe, another one might be on the warpath, and no man could know in advance whether an unexpected encounter would prove harmless or fatal.

There were other enemies—white men who had become outlaws, vengeful, thievish, and often murderous. Those who made the dangerous and arduous crossing from Missouri to California took their lives in their hands. Any man who survived the trip could be justly proud of his achievement.

We can understand, then, how it was that California, admitted as a state into the Union, was nevertheless isolated from the rest of the United States. Under the circumstances, the mails to and from California were bound to be bad—slow, inefficient, uncertain.

It was natural for California to look to Congress for relief. One of its two senators, Senator William McKendree Gwin, had a strategic post on the Senate Committee on Post Offices and Post Roads. Born in Tennessee in 1805, he practiced medicine in his native state and in Mississippi for a time, until President Andrew Jackson appointed him U.S. Marshal for Mississippi. After being elected to Congress from Mississippi, Gwin moved out to California, apparently with the deliberate purpose of getting himself elected senator from the new state.

There were plausible grounds for his ambition. A man of considerable charm, he has been described as "the most intellectual, brilliant, subtle, suave, and unscrupulous leader California ever had." Elected to the First General Assembly in California, Gwin had little trouble establishing his leadership in a group of which two-thirds of the members always went armed with a pistol or knife—preferably both. The assembly elected Gwin to the Senate and then re-elected him in 1857.

For various reasons, Gwin had trouble in making headway in his efforts to promote swift delivery of mail and freight. One obstacle was the fact that much of the thinking in Congress about communications with California was influenced by an erroneous conception of the Southwest as "the Great American Desert."

It was this quaint notion that led to the bizarre introduction of camels by Jefferson Davis in 1853, when he was Secretary of War under President Franklin Pierce. Davis suggested the experiment and Congress made the appropriation in 1855.

The arguments for using camels seemed unassailable. The ability of these animals to withstand thirst and heat in the desert was well known. Their swiftness and hardiness had made them ideal for desert travel for centuries.

At first, they would be used to carry mail and freight, and to maintain swift communications between military posts. A camel corps of scouts could render valuable service in the event that an Indian war broke out. Some military theorist even hit on the idea of setting up a light artillery camel corps. Presumably, the light cannon would be placed between the humps while the artillerymen took shelter behind the animals.

Two naval attachés were instructed to visit the London zoo to learn all about camels, and then to proceed to Arabia to purchase seventy-five camels for $30,000. The Navy furnished a vessel to provide transport for the animals, which were brought to San Antonio for experiment by the Army. In a report issued in August, 1856, Major Wayne, who was in charge of the experiments, stated that "the experiment should show that the dromedaries may be sent anywhere along the frontier or within the settlements. One or more may be mounted with a small gun, throwing shrapnel. These experiments would not only show the absolute value of the animals for burden and the saddle, but also the camel's relative usefulness in comparison with the horse, the mule and waggoning."

The logic was impeccable, and had only one draw-back—it was ludicrously at odds with the facts. The experiments turned out to be miserable failures. Horses and mules were terrified by the presence of the strange animals. The camels quickly developed sore feet on the rough desert terrain which was quite different from the Sahara with its soft, drifting sands. When the camels were shod with leather boots their speed naturally decreased. In any event, they failed to exhibit any superiority over horses and mules. When failure became obvious, they were either sold to circus outfits or allowed to take to the desert. Thus ended one of the most bizarre episodes in American history.

We have seen, then, that while the problem of mail delivery in California had been satisfactorily solved by the "Jackass Express" outfits, the movement of mail across the country proved a much more difficult problem to solve.

For years, the Post Office Department did not handle this mail directly. Instead, it gave out contracts to private individuals and companies to carry mail between the Missouri frontier and California.

All these enterprises were failures for one reason or another—but all suffered from a prime defect: the government's contract payments, with perhaps one exception, were hopelessly inadequate. The contractors were usually public-spirited, conscientious, willing to risk their lives and their money. But without proper support from the government, they could not prosper.

Two mail routes were gradually established. One was comparatively long, but it was not hampered by too much snowfall in wintertime. Known as the Ox-Bow (or Butterfield) Route, it swung south from St. Louis down to Arkansas and through Texas, New Mexico, and Arizona. At Yuma, in Arizona, it forked into two routes, one leading to Los Angeles in southern California and the other going north to San Francisco and the gold fields.

The other main route, further north, was several hundred miles shorter, but it was covered by such deep snows during winter that it was doubtful whether the mail could be carried on it for more than six months of the year. In addition, the westernmost part of this route was made up of very difficult terrain—mountains and deserts. This was the Central Route, pronounced by many experts as out of the question. This, by the way, was the one later selected for the Pony Express!

The government's first mail contract went to Samuel Woodson in 1850, for a monthly service between Salt Lake City and Independence, Missouri. Slow as this schedule was, Woodson was unable to stick to it. Lacking the necessary funds, he failed to establish relay stations along the way to furnish fresh animals; his weary mule teams had to plod the whole way without any relief. Also, the lack of replacement teams made it impossible to keep the service going at the rate of twenty-four hours a day. No wonder Woodson's service was much too slow.

One of the earliest pioneers in using the Central Route was the heroic Major George Chorpenning who, together with his partner Absalom Woodward, signed a contract with the government in 1851. The agreement called for two deliveries a month over the seven hundred-mile distance between Salt Lake City and Sacramento.

In May, 1851, Chorpenning and Woodward loaded their pack mules with mail bags and started eastward from Sacramento. The round trip, which took thirteen months, was dogged by misfortune. On the way, Woodward was murdered by Indians, while Chorpenning was so badly wounded that he could not make the return trip.

Nine months later, in February, 1852, a Chorpenning employee named Edson Cody set out from Sacramento with four men and another pack-mule team. The grueling trip to Salt Lake City took fifty-three days. All their animals froze to death. The men had to proceed on foot, floundering through deep snows.

This meant struggling for two hundred miles, the heavy mail sacks loaded on their backs. The last eleven days were particularly trying; for the first seven of them they had nothing but mule meat to live on, and after that they had no food at all.

Other mail parties met with similar privations. Parties which set out in the spring, for example, were harried by Indians. Generally they succeeded in beating off the attackers, but took serious losses in the process. The upshot was that Chorpenning could get no one to deliver mail for him. In order to safeguard his contracts he came to a desperate decision: he decided to deliver the mail himself, without any companions. It was the resolve of a very brave—or very foolish—man.

We have scant information on how Chorpenning safely delivered the mail from Sacramento to Salt Lake City—rugged country all the way. His escape from

Indian ambush seems a minor miracle. It has been conjectured that he traveled by night and hid during the day. By his courageous act Chorpenning saved his mail contract and kept the Central Overland mail route open. This, as we shall see later on, was an achievement of great historical importance.

Chorpenning renewed his contract with the government which now established a somewhat different route: from Salt Lake it swung southwest and then turned north to Sacramento. The new deliveries were accomplished by pack mules, occasionally by heavy wagon. Again Indian attacks made these trips dangerous, and this called for armed escorts.

In view of these difficulties, it is understandable that the bulk of the mail between California and the eastern seaboard continued to be sent by sea. This method, if somewhat slower, was at least safer. However, the company which handled the ocean-going mail had a monopoly and therefore charged an excessive price.

This aroused a great deal of resentment among Californians who kept clamoring for a more reasonable fee. They felt even more strongly on this point because the government contracts with Chorpenning allowed him such a measly fee that, in addition to the dangers to which he was exposed, he was operating at a loss.

Californians had still another cause for discontent. They were eager to receive books, magazines and above all, newspapers. But such mail was too heavy and bulky to be carried by pack mules. The only alternative was ocean shipping, but here the costs were exorbitant.

At last it was announced that wagon delivery was to be established on the Central Overland Route between Salt Lake City and Placerville, in the heart of the California mining region. Reasonably prompt and economical delivery of bulk mail had finally become feasible. Delivery time, which had been standardized in the neighborhood of thirty days, was now to be reduced to a little over two weeks.

So far Chorpenning had received a niggardly annual governmental fee of about $14,000 a year. Now his new service was to receive about $190,000 a year. To speed up service and make it more reliable, Chorpenning proceeded to build stations every thirty miles or so along the route.

Yet Chorpenning continued to experience crippling money difficulties. Although his investment in the route amounted to some $300,000 the government reduced his fee from $190,000. In May, 1860, the government canceled the contract "for repeated failures, for establishing an inferior grade of stock on said road." Evidently, Chorpenning lacked the right friends to put in a good word for him in Washington. He started a suit against the government which dragged on for years. And so Chorpenning, for all his heroic efforts, disappeared from the picture.

By 1859, mail delivery had reached its lowest point of efficiency. Heavily armed emigrant trains and freight wagons could make the trip safely, but they were maddeningly slow. Nevertheless, the search for satisfactory mail delivery over the Central Overland Route was intensified by the discovery of silver in Nevada, and the discovery of gold in Colorado.

The government's opposition to the Central Overland Route seems mysterious at first glance, but there were very practical reasons underlying the attitude expressed in Congress. During the decade of the 1850s both the North and the South were girding for the coming Civil War. The choice of a government-subsidized mail route became part of this struggle.

Southerners in Congress naturally favored the southerly (Butterfield) route, for in case of civil war it would be comparatively easy for southern forces to seize control of the route. What was really at stake here, as we shall see later on, was control of the great new rich state of California.

While the southern route was fairly free of the difficulties that plagued the Central Overland Route, it was so infested with hostile Indians that some of the mail carriers were killed on the way. The struggle seemed hopeless, but one thing that kept the southern route alive was the outrageous rate charged by the ocean carriers.

It had become clear that government assistance was essential, but here the heartbreaking enterprise became mired in political struggles. When California's Senator Gwin tried to get a bill through Congress to set up a mail line along the Central Route and construct military posts along the way to keep the Indians in check, he ran into southern opposition.

In the political jockeying that followed, the southerners won out. The southern route became the official, subsidized route, with John Butterfield in charge.

The Senate's choice of the southern route had the support of Postmaster General Aaron V. Brown of Tennessee who, naturally, was sympathetic to the southern point of view. Since Senator Gwin was himself a southern sympathizer, it is possible that he did not push his measure as forcefully as he might have.

In the debates on the Butterfield Route, Senator Iverson of Georgia openly appealed to sectional passions in frankly explaining why the South wanted the southerly route:

> They want to take this away from the southern states and put it upon their own region, for the purpose of depriving the South of the poor benefit of having a mail route in the southern states. The object is to operate on the construction line of the Pacific railroad. That is the ultimate design, and is another one of those circumstances in which the northern numerical majority of the government intends to absorb all the benefits of the government. I hope that southern Senators put their foot down on this proposition, and that this amendment, which is nothing less than an attempt to monopolize the benefits of this government for the North, will be voted down.

When the Post Office Department sent a special inspector to study the southern route he reported: "The stations in Arizona are at the mercy of the Apache, and the Comanche may, at his pleasure, bar the passage of stages in Texas." Yet this was the route which was officially designated and paid for by the United States Government!

Butterfield, a friend of President Buchanan, was an experienced man who had successfully run a stagecoach and mail delivery line between Utica and Syracuse in New York state. His new route started with two eastern forks, one beginning from Memphis, the other from St. Louis. Both forks joined at Fort Smith, Arkansas, where the Butterfield Route proper started south.

As a result, the route completely ignored Salt Lake

City and Sacramento, causing furious resentment in those towns. But Postmaster General Brown was never at a loss for a plausible explanation: the choice of the more logical Central Route would not do because the western end was impassable—not to mention the fact that the whole route was menaced by hostile Indians. This was not the whole story, but there was just enough truth in Brown's explanation to carry weight.

Butterfield's mail contract enabled him to provide fairly good stagecoaches which carried as few as nine people and as many as fourteen. Luggage and mail were stowed in the triangular-shaped "boot" in the back of the coach.

But Butterfield's route had its troubles, too. Station keepers were at the mercy of marauding Apaches and Comanches, as we have seen. Traveling was so uncomfortable in the fearfully hot desert summers that many a traveler was heard to remark feelingly that he now knew what hell was like. But the chief reason for discontent was that a round trip took at least 50 days slow travel and slow mail delivery.

The discontent became even greater when gold was discovered in Colorado in 1859, leading to another gold rush. Once more isolated mining camps mushroomed, crowded with lonely men who were eager for news from the East. But the area was hundreds of miles from the Butterfield Route or any other mail route, and the nearest post office at Fort Laramie was two hundred miles away.

At last—at long last—the Pony Express was ready to make its bow.

3 *"Go West, Young Man!"*

THE FAME of Horace Greeley, the editor of the *New York Tribune*, rests on his well-known advice: "Go west, young man!" In 1859, he took his own advice and went west to write a series of articles about the Colorado gold rush. When he stopped off in Leavenworth, Kansas, he was amazed by the scope of the activities carried on by the largest freighting firm on the frontier.

> Russell, Majors & Waddell's transportation establishment, between the fort and the city, is the great feature of Leavenworth. Such acres of wagons; such pyramids of extra axle-trees; such herds of oxen; such regiments of drivers and other employees! No one who does not see can realize how vast a business this is; nor how numerous are its outlays as well as its revenue. I presume this great firm has at this hour two millions of dollars invested in stock, mainly oxen, mules and wagons.

At that time, an average of 500 wagons was passing Fort Kearny daily. In one year, 21,000,000 tons of freight were shipped from Atchison, Kansas. In its heyday, Russell, Majors & Waddell employed over 6,000 men and required 75,000 oxen. Freight rates were high. For example, to send a hundred pounds of flour from Atchison to Denver—a little over 600 miles—cost about $9.

The three men who ran the great firm had vastly different temperaments. Russell was born in 1812 in Vermont and was brought to Missouri in his late teens. He started in business as a storekeeper in Lexington, Missouri, a prosperous little town which profited from the fur trade and commerce along the Santa Fe Trail. In the course of time Russell became well-to-do, which enabled him to purchase valuable real estate.

In 1847, he joined in a venture to send goods to Santa Fe. This was how he got his start in freighting supplies. During the Mexican War his firm shipped military equipment to Santa Fe. Russell became so wealthy that he built a twenty-room mansion and became socially prominent. He helped organize an insurance company and was one of the founders of a college for women. In 1851, Russell entered the freighting firm in which he was to become associated with Majors and Waddell.

Russell was a promoter in the best sense. He was energetic, quick to see opportunities, enthusiastic and determined. At the same time, he enjoyed a fine reputation and was immensely popular.

Alexander Majors hailed from Kentucky where he was born in 1814. He was brought to Missouri in early childhood. Growing up on the frontier, he remained a frontiersman at heart despite his later wealth. After farming for a while, he decided there was little future in it and decided, in 1848, to go into the freighting business.

All his life Majors remained faithful to his stern Presbyterian upbringing. So at the very start he exacted the following pledge from all his freighting employees:

While I am in the employ of A. Majors, I agree
not to use profane language, not to get drunk, not to
gamble, nor to treat the animals cruelly, and not to
do anything incompatible with the conduct of a gentleman. I agree if I violate any of the above conditions to accept my discharge without any pay for my
services.

Majors soon achieved a reputation for integrity which
got him more freighting contracts, including work for
western army posts. As time went on, Majors prospered
steadily. He continued to maintain his principles, picking his employees carefully and treating them well because he himself had lived the kind of hard life they had
to endure.

And because Majors had worked with farm animals
and learned to love them, he continued to insist that
they be well treated. With his high competence in the
freighting business it was natural for him to join forces
with Russell.

The third member of the partnership, William B.
Waddell, was born in Virginia in 1807. His family
moved to Kentucky in 1815. As a young man he moved
to Illinois, then to St. Louis and back to Kentucky. He
tried keeping store and farming for a while, but, like
Majors, he was ambitious and wanted to get into something more enterprising.

In the middle 1830s he went west again, and like
Russell he settled in Lexington, Missouri. Opening a
store to outfit emigrants, he prospered mightily, and in
1853 he formed a freighting partnership with Russell.
In January, 1855, the firm merged with Majors' business and thus the great freighting enterprise came into
existence.

Russell's main activity was representing the firm in the East, where he had entree to government and banking circles. His business ability and easy charm qualified him ideally for such activity.

Majors supervised the freight traffic, a field in which he was thoroughly experienced and able. He was often away from home, traveling over the freight routes and making sure that everything was going satisfactorily.

Waddell handled financial matters and purchases, remaining in charge of the home office. On the whole the partners got on well despite their differences in temperament. Russell was always making big plans and willing to take risks. Majors and Waddell, on the other hand, were conservative, took a long time to come to a decision and shunned long-term commitments.

Since Russell was a man of vision while his partners were more earthbound, he saw superb money-making opportunities in the Colorado gold discovery while they remained unmoved. So, when Russell impetuously proposed to his associates the idea of starting a daily mail coach line from Leavenworth to Denver, they were appalled.

Without a substantial government contract they would have to advance large sums of money. Then there were the difficulties of the mountainous terrain. And finally, wasn't all this rather premature? Who could say how big the gold deposits were? If they gave out, the mining camps would become ghost camps in a short time. Then what would happen to their costly investment? (Actually their fears on this last point were well justified.)

But nothing could hold Russell back. Sooner or later, he reasoned optimistically, the government would supply a contract. Unable to budge his unwilling partners, he joined forces with another Missouri freighter named John Jones to form the Leavenworth and Pike's Peak Express Company.

In the spring of 1859, the new company borrowed enough money to buy fifty handsome, comparatively comfortable coaches and some eight hundred mules. There were daily departures from Leavenworth and Denver, and good meals were served to the passengers at way stations. According to William Larimer:

> The coaches in this service were large, strongly built vehicles, known as Concord coaches. Each one cost about $800 and was especially fitted for the heavy work required of it. Nine passengers could be accommodated with ease inside of each. They were softly cushioned, and in winter were warm and comfortable. They were altogether the finest stages run in the West. Each coach was drawn by four fine, strong Kentucky mules, which were changed every ten to twenty miles. The drivers were well paid, intelligent, experienced and fearless. An accident was a rarity. The stage fare between the Missouri River and Denver was at first $150, but later $100 each way. There were said to be 52 coaches running on the Leavenworth-Denver line.

The charges were quite reasonable—letters cost a quarter, while packages were a dollar a pound. Nevertheless, the company had a large investment to recoup and was soon deep in the red, running a thousand dollar loss a day.

The stagecoach line had been financed on ninety-day notes. The government mail contract never turned up, so when the notes came due they could not be met. But the resourceful Russell was by no means at the end of his tether: he managed to persuade his partners, Majors and Waddell, to take over the ailing coach line.

But the line continued to operate at a loss. In the hope of recouping some of its heavy expenses the partnership transferred some of the coaches to the Central Overland Route to Salt Lake City.

In February, 1860, the line was extended again—this time to California. With coaches that covered 120 miles a day this was a practicable proposition. The partners built many new stations and bought more animals, achieving an efficiency which allowed them to cut down the average trip from twenty-two days to ten days. The line now took on the resounding name of Central Overland California and Pike's Peak Express Company.

But even this new line, which provided satisfactory travel to California for the first time, could not pay its way. The losses went inexorably on. Russell at last realized that enthusiasm and doing a good job were not enough: he would have to work through political channels in Washington. He found a valuable ally in Senator Gwin, who as we know was interested in good mail service to California and was a member of the senatorial committee that could make or break the legislation that Russell needed to keep his firm in business.

Russell and Gwin discussed the problem in Washington. What was needed, said Gwin, was some impressive example of the merits of the Central Route. Whatever was done had to be exciting, colorful—something that would capture the imagination of the people and their representatives.

And Gwin knew just what was needed, he went on.

Back in 1854, he had traveled on horseback along the Central Route, on his way from San Francisco to Washington. (There was a popular joke in those days that a Senator or Congressman from California might find that his term of office was over by the time he reached the nation's capital.) Part of the way he had traveled with B. F. Ficklin, general superintendent of Russell, Majors & Waddell.

Few men had Ficklin's experience in the field of overland transportation. Above all he was ambitious to create much faster communication between California and Missouri. He had worked out a plan for a faster mail service, and knowing that the senator was interested, he told Gwin what he had in mind.

As he had foreseen, Gwin was fascinated—partly because he was eager to see California benefit from a rapid mail service, partly because he would obtain a political advantage from the credit he would gain from making the mail plan feasible.

Ficklin had still another reason for confiding in Gwin. With his experience, he realized at once that his plan would be too costly to be operated profitably by a private firm, no matter how rich it might be, unless it had financial support from the government.

Senator Gwin agreed to do his part, but as we know, his plan was scuttled by southern senators. And Gwin, because of his southern sympathies, was later to withdraw his support for the Central Route. But at the time of his conversations with Russell, Gwin was still enthusiastically in favor of the idea.

No sooner did Russell hear of this concept of a "Pony Express" than he was wholeheartedly in favor of it. The idea, so bold and far-reaching, was bound to attract this born promoter. Instead of waiting to start the Pony Express after he received government support, he decided to start it at once on condition that Gwin should bend all his efforts to getting a mail contract for the company.

After all, he reasoned, the company had an ample number of way stations which could be used by the Pony Express. Westward from Salt Lake City, to be sure, it would be necessary to construct new stations and stables.

Brimming over with enthusiasm, Russell returned to the home office to broach the idea to his partners. They heard him out glumly. Earlier attempts had failed miserably. The Indian menace was more serious than ever. The winter snows would make the trails impassable. The Postmaster General had tersely delivered his opinion on the subject of mail delivery via the Central Overland Route: "Out of the question."

The likelihood of failure and sizeable losses was overwhelming. But Russell was so enthusiastic and so forceful that he carried his dubious partners along. Their forebodings of disaster were well-founded. Nevertheless in the process they wrote a glorious chapter in American history.

As soon as the company's plans were announced, hundreds of applicants thronged its offices despite the rigorous requirements for becoming a Pony Express rider. These youngsters, who were no strangers to the hard life of the frontier, were skilled horsemen and hunters, accustomed to dealing with Indians, self-reliant and resourceful. Above all they were drawn by the spirit of adventure.

The firm's agents bought the choicest horses they

could find, in some cases paying triple the cost of an ordinary horse. The efficiency of the Pony Express, and sometimes the very life of its riders, would depend on the spirit, intelligence and endurance of the horses.

Years later, Greene Majors, one of Alexander Majors' sons, described the opening organization of the Pony Express in this way:

> To establish the Pony Express required 500 of the best blooded American horses; one hundred and ninety stock stallions for changing the riding stock; two hundred station tenders to care for the horses and have saddled for the incoming rider and be off like the wind; 80 of the keenest, toughest and bravest of western youths for the riders, with stations all supplied with hay, grain and other needed materials. It required $100,000 in gold coin to establish and equip the line.

For the rugged terrain of the Far West, California mustangs were most suitable. In his reminiscences, *A Senator of the Fifties,* Jeremiah Lynch gave this remarkable instance of their endurance:

> Only a year prior to the gold discovery, Colonel Fremont was hastily summoned from Los Angeles to Monterey. Leaving the former place at early dawn with two companions, he rode 125 miles before halting for the night. They had nine horses as a *caballada* [spare horses] driving six ahead of them, running loose on the trail, and changing every 20 miles.
>
> The second day they made 125 miles. On the third day they did not start until eleven o'clock, yet traveled 80 miles, and on the fourth day they dashed into

Monterey at 3 o'clock, having ridden 90 miles since morning and 420 miles in four days.

Fremont and his party left on their return the next day at four of the afternoon, galloping forty miles that afternoon, 120 miles the next day and 130 miles on the two succeeding days, arriving in Los Angeles on the ninth day from their departure.

They traveled a rough and unpeopled trail. Their actual time in the saddle was 76 hours, and their average was eleven miles an hour. Fremont rode 130 miles in 24 hours on one horse.

The California horses are small, but with deep withers and broad flanks. Except in weight and color they much resemble the Arabian stallions to be seen in the streets of Cairo.

In view of the ancestry of the mustangs, this kinship with the Arabian horses may not be so fanciful as it seems. The word "mustang" comes from the Spanish *mestengo*, meaning "wild." The California mustangs were descended from the Spanish horses brought by the *Conquistadores* to the New World in the fifteenth and sixteenth century. Many of these animals must have been pure-bred Arabian horses.

Whether or not Russell was aware of historical precedents, earlier post-horse systems had always emphasized the choice of first-class mounts for their riders. Before we study the Pony Express operations in detail, it would be interesting to learn something about these earlier systems.

4 The Pony Express and Its Forerunners

As a **PROGRESSIVE**, energetic, and far-seeing American businessman, William Russell would undoubtedly have been astounded if someone had told him that his Pony Express was modeled in many ways on the post-horse system of Darius the Great, who reigned over the Persian Empire 2500 years ago. His domains extended from Egypt in the west to the shores of the Black Sea in the east; and from the Danube River in the north to the Indian Ocean in the south.

The Roman Empire, with its magnificent network of fine roads, also had an efficient courier system which assured rapid communications. The finest post-horse system of all was the one organized by Kublai Khan (the Great Khan) in thirteenth-century China. In 1464, the king of France had post stations built throughout the country for an effective mail-delivery system.

The methods of Darius deserve some attention because we have to marvel at the efficiency he achieved at so early a point in time. As he ruled over twenty provinces extending over a vast area, Darius was always absorbed in the problem of having excellent communications. He had many highways built from Susa, his capital, to the provincial capitals. We can get some idea of the extent of his road construction from the fact that the highway from Susa to Sardis was fifteen hundred miles long.

At every fifteen miles, according to Herodotus, "There are royal stations and excellent inns, and the whole road is through an inhabited and safe country." Each station was always provided with a relay of fresh horses. Thus, while it took the ordinary traveler three months to get from Susa to Sardis, the royal mail covered the same distance in ten days!

Ferries were an important part of the system, though the most important rivers, such as the Euphrates, were bridged by structures so substantial that hundreds of elephants could be safely taken across them at one time. Even at the outermost borders—at the Afghanistan mountain passes into India, for example—Darius had splendid roads built.

His communications system thus assured tight administrative control and quick military movements. It also fostered commerce and the lively exchange of ideas and customs that enrich a civilization.

The communications system of the Romans was perhaps even more remarkable. Their road-building was so magnificent that nothing equal to their highways appeared in Europe until the coming of the railroad. In Italy alone there were over 370 main routes and some twelve thousand miles of paved road. It is thought that the whole empire had over fifty thousand miles of paved highways—not counting thousands of miles for the paved local roads. From the city of Rome splendid roads radiated to Paris, Bordeaux, Cologne, Utrecht, Vienna and literally hundreds of other cities.

Most amazing of all was the amount of planning and forethought that went into the communications network. Thousands of superb bridges were built. On the great consular roads there was a stone marker at every mile to show the distance to the next town. Even today four thousand of these markers are still in existence. At suitable intervals there were stone seats to enable tired travelers to rest.

At every ten miles there was a *statio* where fresh horses could be obtained; at intervals of thirty miles there was a *mansio*—an inn which had a shop and a bar. In the cities there were hotels which were sometimes owned by the municipal government.

The public stagecoaches made about 60 miles a day. The official post-horse system operated on a 24-hour basis, covering about a hundred miles a day. However, the imperial messengers who brought the news of Nero's death to Spain to Galba—the next emperor—made 332 miles in 36 hours. The post-horse system owed a great deal to the emperor Augustus, who consciously modeled the system on that of Darius, and for the same reason— more efficient administration. The system was used only for official mail, though on rare occasions prominent individuals might gain permission to use the official posts.

The Romans also had a semaphore system of a very rudimentary kind which could be flashed from point to point, ultimately covering quite a distance. The semaphore was used, for example, to signal the arrival of grain ships at a time when the supply was running low.

But the distinction of establishing the finest post-horse system belongs to Kublai Khan, who reigned as emperor of China from about 1215 to 1294. Marco Polo, who spent several years at the emperor's court, left a fascinating account of the Chinese system.

From the city of Kanbalu, there are many roads leading to the different provinces, and upon each of these, that is to say, upon every great high road, at the distance of 25 or 35 miles, accordingly as the towns happen to be situated, there are stations with houses of accommodation for travelers. These are called *yamb* or post-houses. They are large and handsome buildings, having several well-furnished apartments, hung with silk, and provided with everything suitable to persons of rank. Even kings may be lodged at these stations in a becoming manner, as every article required may be obtained from the towns and strong places in the vicinity; and for some of them the court makes regular provisions.

At each station 400 good horses are kept in constant readiness, in order that all messengers going and coming upon the business of the Great Khan, and all ambassadors, may have relays, and, leaving their jaded horses, be supplied with fresh ones. Even in mountainous districts, remote from the great roads, where there are no villages, and the towns are far distant from each other, His Majesty has equally caused buildings of the same kind to be erected, furnished with everything necessary, and provided with the usual supply of horses.

He sends people to dwell upon the spot, in order to cultivate the land, and attend to the service of the post; by which means large villages are formed. In consequence of these regulations, ambassadors to the court, and the royal messengers, go and return through every province and kingdom of the empire with the greatest convenience and facility. In the management of all this the Great Khan exhibits a superiority over every other emperor, king, or human being.

In his dominions no fewer than 200,000 horses are thus employed in the department of the post, and 10,000 buildings, with suitable furniture, are kept up.

It must be understood, however, that of the four hundred horses the whole are not constantly on service at the station, but only two hundred, which are kept there for the space of a month. During this period the other half are at pasture; and at the beginning of the month, these in turn take the duty, whilst the former have time to recover their flesh; each alternately relieving the other.

When it is necessary that the messengers should proceed with extraordinary despatch, as in the case of giving information of disturbance in any part of the country, the rebellion of a chief, or other important matter, they ride two hundred, or sometimes two hundred and fifty miles in the course of a day. On such occasions they carry with them the tablet of the gerfalcon as a signal of the urgency of their business and the necessity for despatch. And when there are two messengers, they take their departure together from the same place, mounted upon good fleet horses; and they gird their bodies tight, bind a cloth round their heads, and push their horses to the greatest speed. They continue thus till they come to the next post-house, at 25 miles distant, where they find two other horses, fresh and in a state for work; they spring upon them without taking any repose, and changing in the same manner at every stage, until the day closes, they perform a journey of two hundred and fifty miles.

In cases of great emergency they continue their course during the night, and if there should be no moon, they are accompanied to the next station by persons on foot, who run before them with lights; when of course they do not make the same speed as in the daytime, the light-bearers not being able to exceed a certain pace. Messengers qualified to undergo this extraordinary degree of fatigue are held in high estimation.

When we compare the efficiency of the thirteenth-century system of the Great Khan with that of the Pony Express, we have to admit that Kublai Khan comes off very well. But he had great advantages: he had all the resources of the empire behind him, and he operated with virtually unlimited funds. The Pony Express, on the other hand, never got a penny of state support, and it had to scrimp along on borrowed capital. In addition, the empire had splendid roads, whereas the terrain on which the Pony Express functioned was a built-in source of trouble and hardship. When these handicaps are taken into consideration, the Pony Express does not come off too badly.

As originally planned by Russell, the Pony Express was to have eighty expert, lightweight riders; four hundred fast and hardy horses; and eighty relay stations. Proceeding west from St. Joseph, the route would continue over the prairies, then up the Platte and Sweetwater rivers to South Pass, across the Rockies to Salt Lake City in mountainous Utah, into the Nevada deserts, and finally across the Sierra Nevada Mountains into California.

It was rugged country all the way, calling for the utmost stamina in horses and riders. The stations would require some four hundred men to ward off Indian attacks and maintain provisions and shelter for the Pony Express riders and their mounts.

Originally Russell proposed that the government pay him five hundred dollars per round trip for two trips a week in both directions. But he greatly underestimated the costs involved, which actually turned out to be about fifteen times what Russell had calculated.

Since the Pony Express messengers would have to depend on fast riding to escape from Indian attack, each animal's load was limited to 165 pounds. This allowed 20 pounds for the mail, 25 pounds for the equipment and 120 pounds for the rider.

Many of the youngsters who joined the Pony Express had been brought up on ranches in the Missouri area. They were expert riders by the time they were 14— light, wiry and accustomed to being in the saddle for hours without fatigue.

The most famous of them was John W. Richardson who was to do the first relay from St. Joseph to get the Pony Express off to a fast start, and the last to come in at St. Joseph with a view to making up for time lost at an earlier stage on the homeward trip.

The mail was carried in a *mochila*—a leather cover that fitted snugly over the saddle and could be put on and removed very easily. Each corner of the *mochila* had a pouch with a lock. The keys to open these pouches were kept only in St. Joseph (the eastern terminal), Salt Lake City and Sacramento (the western terminal).

For the difficult mountain and desert country west of the Rockies the Pony Express used, as we have seen, hardy mustangs specially picked for endurance. Fast horses were chosen for the prairie country, where speedy riding could be anticipated. In the west, about 160 miles a day was the maximum expected. In the eastern section, on the other hand, about 220 miles a day seemed a reasonable goal.

From the start it was all too obvious that the conditions for riding as a Pony Express messenger would be hard and dangerous. But so many adventurous young men were eager to take on the assignment that Russell, Majors & Waddell could have hired them for a very small sum. Instead they decided to pay the riders over a hundred dollars a month—very generous wages for those days.

Yet the Pony Express riders' money would not have gone very far in California if they had had to buy their own meals. Although the price of food had decreased considerably from what had been the going rates during the gold-rush days, it was still quite steep. A wedge of pie, for example, sold for seventy-five cents in California, while back in the East it was five cents—or less.

But money was not the firm's only concern. Every rider had to sign the following pledge, composed by Majors, before he was hired:

I do hereby swear, before the Great and Living God, that during my engagement, and while I am an employee of Russell, Majors & Waddell, I will, under no circumstances, use profane language; that I will drink no intoxicating liquors; that I will not quarrel or fight with any other employee of the firm, and that in every respect I will conduct myself honestly, be faithful to my duties, and so direct all my acts as to win the confidence of my employers. So help me God.

When a Pony Express rider was hired he received a lightweight rifle and a Colt revolver. But these were strictly for defense. The riders were sternly forbidden to take the offensive against Indians or other enemies. Each rider also received a distinctive costume—a gaudy red shirt and blue pants.

A horn, to be blown on approaching a station, completed his outfit. This was intended as a time-saving device. On hearing the horn blown, the relay-station keeper and his stableman would get his next mount ready. Every second counted, for the change of horses was scheduled to take place in no more than two minutes.

Each rider was also given a Bible. But the life of a Pony Express rider was so exacting that the boys must have had to wait for their retirement to find the time to read the Scriptures.

The Pony Express made it possible to send news items and business reports much more rapidly between California and Europe. Englishmen, Frenchmen and Germans were fascinated by this romantic, adventurous group. The *London Illustrated News* sent one of its crack reporters to prepare a very detailed report on the Pony Express. The first article of the series was prefaced by this note:

Some of our readers may possibly be puzzled, when reading American news, to find most important intelligence from California, Oregon, British Columbia and the Pacific side of North America contained in a short paragraph headed "By Pony Express"; and the question naturally arises, what is meant by a Pony Express? where does it come from? where does it go? and why is it a Pony Express and not a horse, or a stagecoach, or a railway express? For the purpose of giving some information on this point, our correspondent has taken the trouble to visit the locale of the Pony Express, to see it arrive and depart at its eastern terminus, and also to get a view of it en route on the plains.

French and German newspapers followed suit. Dime novels full of fanciful adventures were very popular in Europe. Richard Burton, another British correspondent on his way west to write about the Mormons, also followed the Pony Express routes. Burton, who a few years earlier had a hand in the sensational discovery of the mysterious source of the Nile, was naturally proud of being an Englishman; so his chimney-pot hat, his frock coat and his silk umbrella accompanied him to the prairies and the Rockies. The high price of transporting his voluminous luggage left him characteristically unruffled. "As you value your nationality," this illustrious tenderfoot advised his stay-at-home countrymen, "let no false shame cause you to forget your hat box and umbrella."

On his travels Burton made a sketch of an Arapahoe Indian to see whether the Indians took offense at this as he had found the African natives did. According to

Burton, the Indian merely grunted in a presumably un-complimentary manner and walked away in dudgeon when shown his portrait. Another version has it that the Indian was so enraged that together with some com-rades he attacked a stagecoach.

Burton's description of his encounter with a Pony Express rider is certainly in the great western tradition of the tall story:

> I preferred to correct my Shoshonee vocabulary under the inspection of Mose Wright, a Pony Express rider from a neighboring station. None of your "one-horse" interpreters, he had learned the difficult dia-lect in his youth, and had acquired all the intonation of an Indian. Educated beyond the reach of civiliza-tion, he was in these days an oddity. He was con-victed of having mistaken a billiard cue for a whip handle, and was accused of having mounted the post supporting an electric telegraph wire in order to hear what it was saying.

> On a later occasion he again caught up with Mose Wright, "who again kindly assisted me in correcting my vocabulary." A delightful scene this must have made!

The most famous description of a Pony Express rider, however, came not from a foreigner but from an American. Mark Twain left his native town of Han-nibal, Missouri as a young man to go west. In *Roughing It,* he described in humorous yet realistic fashion the hard life of the mining camps. In the quotation which follows, he tells how eagerly he and his fellow pas-sengers in a stagecoach hoped to get a glimpse of a Pony Express rider:

In a little while all interest was taken up in stretching our necks and watching for the "pony-rider"— the fleet messenger who sped across the continent from St. Joe to Sacramento, carrying letters 1,900 miles in eight days! Think of that for perishable horse and human flesh and blood to do!

The pony-rider was usually a little bit of a man, brimful of spirit and endurance. No matter what time of the day or night his watch came on, and no matter whether it was winter or summer, raining, snowing, hailing or sleeting, or whether his "beat" was a level straight road or a crazy trail over mountain crags and precipices, or whether it led through peaceful regions or regions that swarmed with hostile Indians, he must always be ready to leap into the saddle and be off like the wind!

There was no idling-time for a pony-rider on duty. He rode 50 miles without stopping, by daylight, moonlight, starlight, or through the blackness of darkness—just as it happened.

He rode a splendid horse that was born for a racer and fed and lodged like a gentleman; kept him at his utmost speed for ten miles, and then, as he came crashing up to the station where stood two men holding fast a fresh, impatient steed, the transfer of rider and mailbag was made in a twinkling of an eye, and away flew the eager pair and were out of sight before the spectator could get hardly the ghost of a look.

The stagecoach traveled about a hundred to 125 miles a day (24 hours), and pony-rider about 250. There were about 80 pony-riders in the saddle all the time, night and day, stretching in a long, scattering procession from Missouri to California, 40 flying eastward, and 40 to the west, and among them making 400 gallant horses earn a stirring livelihood and see a great deal of scenery every single day in the year.

We had a consuming desire, from the beginning, to see a pony-rider, but somehow or other all that passed us and all that met us managed to streak by us in the night, and so we heard only a whiz and a hail, and the swift phantom of the desert was gone before we could get our heads out of the windows. But now we were expecting one along every moment, and we would see him in broad daylight. Presently the driver exclaims: "Here he comes!"

Every neck is stretched further, and every eye strained wider. Away across the endless dead level of the prairie a black speck appears against the sky, and it is plain that it moves. Well, I should think so! In a second or two it becomes a horse and rider, rising nearer—growing more and more defined—nearer and nearer, and the flutter of the hoofs comes faintly to the ear—another instant a whoop and a hurrah from our own upper deck, a wave of the rider's hand, but no reply, and man and horse burst past our excited faces, and go winging away like a belated fragment of a storm!

So sudden is it all, and so like a flash of unreal fancy, that but for the flake of white foam left quivering and perishing on a mail-sack after the vision had flashed by and disappeared, we might have doubted whether we had seen any actual horse and man at all, maybe.

Thus the saga of the Pony Express was immortalized in the vivid prose of Mark Twain.

5 *"They're Off!"*

APRIL 3, 1860, remains a memorable day in the history of the frontier, for that was the day on which the Pony Express began its operations—westward from St. Joseph and eastward from San Francisco. Even in those days San Francisco had already become the most important city in California, but the modern reader may wonder why the town of St. Joseph in Missouri was selected as the eastern terminus.

When the gold rush of '49 started, St. Joseph was a straggling frontier town on the Missouri River with a population of a thousand or so people. But it flourished mightily and grew rapidly when it played host to fifty thousand gold seekers, selling them animals, equipment and supplies of all kinds.

St. Joseph's prosperity came from its strategic location. The emigrants took the ferry across the Missouri into Kansas and then followed a northwest course into Nebraska to the banks of the Platte River. This was the first and easiest stage of the way west.

Later on, when gold was discovered in Colorado, St. Joseph again served as the point of departure for the Colorado mining camps. Once more the fortune seeker ferried across the Missouri into Kansas and this time headed due west for Colorado. Because of its highly favorable location St. Joseph acquired a double advantage—it became a junction of the railroad and stagecoach lines. It served as the westernmost terminal of the railroad lines and the easternmost headquarters of the stage lines.

As the date set for the opening of the Pony Express service approached, more than thirty of the riders checked in at the Patee House in St. Joseph. This was one of the most luxurious hotels of its day, built at a cost of $200,000.

Until the 1960 Centennial, experts differed on whether Johnny Frey or Billy Richardson was the first rider out of St. Joseph. Research proved conclusively that the first was John W. "Billy" Richardson. He was dressed for the occasion—red blouse, blue trousers; gloves, boots, saddle and bridle bespangled with silver and embroidery. The brass band blared, and town officials gave speeches on the importance of the Pony Express.

On this first trip westward from St. Joseph, the Hannibal and St. Joseph Railroad was to deliver mail from the East which was to be carried to California by the Pony Express. Up to this time the mail had been going to St. Joseph by boat; the government had not closed any mail contract with a railroad. So the management of the new railroad was eager to show Uncle Sam what could be done. Years later, the *New York Sun* published a delightful account of the train's adventurous trip to St. Joseph:

Every man on the line considered himself an important part in the event. George H. Davis, the roadmaster, issued orders for every switch to be spiked and all trains kept off the main line. He was selected to make the run, with a nervy engineer, "Ad" Clark, at the throttle.

Clark was a fine specimen of the early-day engineer. He was absolutely fearless. His fame rested mainly on his ability to get his train over the line without mishap. In those days that was a great achievement if running at a high rate of speed. The light rails were easily thrown out of line by heavy rains and the roadbed was no firmer than a country highway.

The mail car used on the run of the Pony Express was the first car constructed for mail purposes in the United States. The engine, named "The Missouri," was a wood burner. From an artistic standpoint it was a much handsomer machine than the big black Moguls of today. There was scrollwork about the headlight, bill and drivers, and all the steel and brass parts were polished until they resembled a looking-glass.

Fuel agents all along the line were notified to be on hand with an adequate force to load the tender in less than no time. The orders given to Engineer Clark were simple. He was to make a speed record to stand for fifty years.

The train pulled out of Hannibal amid the waving of hats and the cheering of a big crowd. All the way across the state, at every station and crossroad it was greeted by enthusiasts, many of whom had journeyed miles to see it. Nothing in northern Missouri had ever excited greater interest.

The first 70 miles of the journey were comparatively level and straight. Through Monroe and Shelby Counties the eager railway officials figured that the little train was making over 60 miles an hour. At Macon it began to strike the rough country, where hills and curves were numerous.

It stopped at Macon for wood. The fuel agent,

L. S. Coleman, had erected a platform, just the height of the tender. On this spot he put every man that could find room, each bearing an armful of selected wood. As the train slowed up, the men emptied their arms. The fuel agent, watch in hand, counted the seconds. Just 15 seconds passed while the train was at a standstill. Then it was off again, like the wind. The spectators saw the occupants of the car clutching their seats with both hands as it rocked to and fro and threatened to toss them all in a heap on the floor.

Out at Macon at that time was a steep grade running down to the Chariton River. If Clark shut off his steam ever so little on that stretch, none of those on board recollect anything about it. If the man at the throttle were alive today he could look with grim satisfaction at the record he made down that hill. That part of the run, at least, has never been beaten by any engineer who has been in the company's employ.

It was like an avalanche. If there had been a tenderfoot on board, a more than reasonable doubt would have arisen in his mind as to whether all the wheels of the train were on the track or not. The furnace was drawing magnificently. A streak of fire shot out of the stack, and the wood sparks flew through the air like snowflakes.

Across the Chariton River there came the New Cambria Hill, a still greater grade than that down from Macon. The momentum attained served to drive the train halfway up with scarcely any perceptible reduction in speed, but the exhausts became slower before the peak of the grade was approached. The fireman piled his dry cottonwood, and the safety valve sent a column of steam heavenward. The white-faced passengers breathed easier, but the relief did not last long. The summit of the hill was reached and the little engine snorted as something alive, took the bit in its teeth, and was soon rushing along at top speed.

When the train pulled in and stopped, Engineer Clark stepped majestically from his iron horse, looking mussed up, grimy and grand. For the present, he was the hero of the hour. He had made the run from Hannibal to St. Joseph, 206 miles, in four hours and 51 minutes—a feat hitherto regarded as impossible. Everybody wanted to shake hands with the keen-eyed man who had done this great thing. It was up to blood and muscle to take up the burden where fire, steam and mechanical skill had left off.

Despite all this rush and bustle the train was late, which meant that the Pony Express would be getting off to a delayed start from St. Joseph. When the train finally arrived, the mail was wrapped in oil silk and put in the *mochila*. The mail consisted of forty-nine letters, five telegrams and some St. Joseph newspapers. For once the western towns would be receiving some fairly fresh news.

A St. Joseph paper, the *Weekly West,* gives us a good idea of the enthusiasm of the townspeople over the start of the Pony Express:

At a quarter past seven last evening, the mail was placed by Mayor Jeff Thompson on the back of the animal, a fine bay mare, who is to run the first stage of the great through express from St. Joseph to her sister cities of the Pacific shore. Horse and rider started off amid the loud and continuous cheers of the assembled multitude, all anxious to witness every particular of the inauguration of this, the greatest enterprise it has become our pleasant duty, as a public journalist, to chronicle.

The Pony Express rider was off, but first he had to cross the Missouri by ferry. This gave him time to discard his fancy costume and put on working clothes. Once on land he galloped off briskly to make up for lost time. After changing his mount four times at way-stations, he dismounted at Granada, Kansas. Having made up almost an hour of lost time, he gave way to his replacement, Don Rising.

Don took an old military road that led right through the reservation of the Kickapoo Indians. He anticipated no trouble and had none, for the Kickapoos were peaceful, friendly farmers who got on well with the white man. Don soon came to Seneca, Kansas, which had the only inn for many miles around—Smith's Hotel. Despite its modest accommodations, it enjoyed a certain fame because its excellent cooking and genial hospitality made it a very welcome resting place for weary travelers on the frontier.

It did not take Don long to arrive at his home station in the town of Marysville, Kansas. This was an important stop on the Oregon Trail. Here Don was replaced by Jack Keetley, a famous Pony Express rider. Out of Marysville the trail was heavy with emigrant trains, so Jack had to be prepared to ride around the wagon trains to avoid losing a lot of time. He wound up at the Cottonwood Station, which also had a general store and a post office.

The prairie was now giving way to beautiful woodlands, in turn to give way to many miles of sagebrush as the rider entered the country of the Platte River, a very peculiar river. In spring it flooded wildly, in summer it all but dried up.

The welcome sight of the Stars and Stripes flying in the breeze told the Pony Express rider that he was at last approaching Fort Kearny in Nebraska, which had been built to protect emigrants on the Oregon Trail. After leaving the fort, he found himself in buffalo country. He passed many Indian lodges, for the Indians liked to camp here in their portable tepees where there was good hunting for buffalo and antelope. About a hundred miles out of Fort Kearny he came to his home station at Cottonwood Springs, an important post for the stagecoach route as well as for the Pony Express.

Gradually, the Pony Express route approached the Rockies. Fort Laramie appeared in sight. This was an outstanding trading post, a popular meeting place of trappers, Indians and emigrants. After fording the Platte, travelers approached one of the famous landmarks of the West—Independence Rock.

Soon the trail would approach South Pass—the gateway through the Rockies to the southern fork of the route In Utah most of the Pony Express riders were Mormon boys, as they naturally were the most familiar with this difficult terrain.

On April 9, the Pony Express rider galloped into Salt Lake City. This was an exciting experience for the townsmen, who could now expect to get news from

Washington in only a week instead of two months—or more.

The seven hundred miles west of Salt Lake provided some of the toughest riding that the Pony Express encountered—broken, twisted mountains and canyons. In some places there was a critical lack of water; other parts of the trail went through Indian country, which could be a serious liability if the Indians were in a hostile mood.

The arrival of the first Pony Express rider from the East aroused the wildest jubilation in Sacramento. Here is how the *Sacramento Union* described the occasion:

> Yesterday's proceedings, impromptu though they were, will long be remembered in Sacramento. The more earnest part of the "Pony" welcome had been arranged earlier in the day. This was the cavalcade of citizens to meet the little traveler a short distance from the city and escort him into town. Accordingly, late in the day, a deputation of about 80 persons, together with a deputation of the Sacramento Hussars assembled at the old Fort, and stretched out their lines on either side along the road along which the Express was to come.
>
> Meanwhile the excitement had increased all over the city. The balconies of the stores were occupied by ladies, and the roofs and sheds were taken possession of by the more agile of the opposite sex, straining to catch a glimpse of the "Pony."
>
> At length—5:45—all this preparation was rewarded. First a cloud of rolling dust in the direction of the Fort, then a horseman, bearing a small flag, riding furiously down J Street, and then a straggling,

charging band of horsemen flying after him, heralding the coming of the Express.

A cannon, placed on the square at Tenth Street, sent forth its noisy welcome. Amidst the firing and shouting, and waving of hats and ladies' handkerchiefs, the pony was seen coming down J Street, surrounded by about 30 of the citizen deputation. Out of this confusion emerged the Pony Express, trotting up to the door of the agency and depositing its mail in ten days from St. Joseph to Sacramento. Hip, hip, hurrah for the Pony Carrier!

The start of the Pony Express from San Francisco on April 3, was equally festive. When the first rider left the city the *Alta Telegraph* published this report:

The first Pony Express started yesterday afternoon, from the Alta Telegraph Company on Montgomery Street. The saddle bags were duly lettered "Overland Pony Express," and the horse (a wiry little animal) was dressed with miniature flags. He proceeded, just before four o'clock, to the Sacramento boat, and was loudly cheered by the crowd as he started. . . . The express matter amounted to 85 letters, which at $5 per letter gave a total receipt of $425.

Actually, the rider, a James Randall, was not a Pony Express rider but a messenger who rode only three blocks to the waterfront where he boarded the steamer for Sacramento with San Francisco's part of the mail.

In the early days of the gold rush it had quickly become clear that a prospective miner could get to the diggings most conveniently by taking a boat passage on the Sacramento River. In this way he bypassed all the hardships of traveling through mountainous territory. Stern-wheel steamers took the newcomers to Sacramento, which had become the capital of the mining district. The city had mushroomed very near the site of Sutter's fort and soon became the purchasing headquarters for miners' equipment and gear.

The result of all this activity was that Sacramento became the important mail center of the Far West. Mail from the East was delivered overland to Sacramento and then went by steamer to San Francisco. Going eastward from San Francisco, mail was brought to Sacramento, and here the Pony Express rider started his arduous and hazardous trip.

History gives Sam Hamilton the honor of being the first eastbound rider. His route was from Sacramento to Sportsman's Hall, a distance of about sixty miles.

Warren Upson, sometimes known as "Boston," was the second rider. His route, from Sportsman's Hall to Friday's Station on the Nevada-California border, took him over the treacherous Sierra Nevada Mountains.

The outdoors was Warren's passion. The Mexican *vaqueros* were magnificent horsemen, but after Warren had learned everything they had to teach him he surpassed them. He also excelled as a marksman. With these qualifications and his love of adventure, Warren Upson was the ideal man for crossing the Sierras.

Warren's first trip was to be a searching test, for the mountain trails were still covered with heavy snows and a fresh storm was in progress. In selecting his pony he was less interested in speed than in picking an animal that was steady and sure-footed. The difficulties had certainly not been exaggerated, for the wagon tracks had been hidden by snowfalls, which likewise concealed many of the familiar landmarks on which Warren had hoped to rely.

There were times when Warren had to get off his horse and lead it cautiously near the sides of canyons where one misstep would mean death. Other times, he was half blinded by the snow coming down from the lowering skies and the loose snow being swept up at him by powerful winds. Under these conditions Warren went on from station to station, without the blizzard letting up. At last he arrived at his home station at Friday's Station, Nevada.

At Friday's Station, Upson was relieved by "Pony Bob" Haslam, probably the greatest Pony Express rider. Haslam's route, terminating at Fort Churchill, Nevada, meant crossing the perilous Great Basin country. The hundred or more mountain ranges of the area were monotonously lacking in real differences and were dangerous to traverse. The rivers, which often served as natural guides, were hard to follow; the Pony Express rode along the Humboldt or Carson as far as possible, but these often disappeared in "sinks" and were lost. Only the most highly skilled could expect to find their way successfully through this maze.

The route the Pony Express finally chose was only a series of lesser evils. A great deal of criticism came from "experts" who felt they could have done better. Nevertheless, on the first westbound trip through this dangerous country, Haslam made his ride to Friday's Station on schedule and without incident. There he turned the *mochila* over to Warren Upson.

The way back was westward over the Sierras where Warren had to thread his way through twenty-foot drifts. Many wagon trains carrying provisions for the miners were out on the trail. In order to make good time Warren often had to gallop around them—a very dangerous thing to do on the narrow mountain trails. And yet he managed to arrive in Placerville, California on time. If such trips had been made once or twice, they would have been remembered as heroic epics. But because they were all in the day's work for a Pony Express rider we tend to take them as a matter of course.

At Sportsman's Hall, Warren handed over the *mochila* to Sam Hamilton. When Sam reached Sacramento he received a hero's welcome, which pleased him but annoyed him too, for he was losing valuable time in getting to the river steamer which was to take him to San Francisco.

Here again he was given an enthusiastic welcome, with speeches, band music, torchlight processions with fire engines, and much cheering and booming of cannon. No wonder the people of San Francisco rejoiced; their isolation from the rest of the country was over.

The people of Salt Lake City were equally thrilled at the prospect of rapid communication. The *Deseret News* of that city gave this report on April 11:

The first Pony Express from the West left Sacramento at 12 p.m. on the night of the 3rd inst., and arrived on the night of the 7th, inside of prospectus time. The roads were heavy, the weather stormy. The last 75 miles were made in five hours and 15 minutes in a heavy rain.

The Express from the east left St. Joseph, Mo. at 6:30 p.m. on the evening of the 3rd and arrived in this city at 6:25 p.m. on the evening of the 9th. The difference in time between this city and St. Joseph is

Sacramento cheers the arrival of the first Pony Express rider.

PONY EXPRESS!

CHANGE OF

TIME!

REDUCED

RATES!

10 Days to San Francisco!

LETTERS

WILL BE RECEIVED AT THE

OFFICE, 84 BROADWAY,

NEW YORK,

Up to **4** P. M. every TUESDAY,

AND

Up to **2½** P. M. every SATURDAY,

Which will be forwarded to connect with the PONY EXPRESS leaving
ST. JOSEPH, Missouri,

Every WEDNESDAY and SATURDAY at 11 P. M.

TELEGRAMS

Sent to Fort Kearney on the mornings of MONDAY and FRIDAY, will connect with **PONY** leaving St. Joseph, WEDNESDAYS and SATURDAYS.

EXPRESS CHARGES.

LETTERS weighing half ounce or under..............**$1 00**
For every additional half ounce or fraction of an ounce 1 00
In all cases to be enclosed in 10 cent Government Stamped Envelopes,
And all Express CHARGES Pre-paid.

☞ **PONY EXPRESS ENVELOPES For Sale at our Office.**

WELLS, FARGO & CO., Ag'ts.

New York, July 1, 1861.

Posters advertised the speed and economy of Pony Express
service.

something near one hour and 15 minutes, bringing us within six days' communication with the frontier, and seven days from Washington—a result which we, accustomed to receive news three months after date, can well appreciate.

(This emphasis on time, right down to the very last minute, may seem like dull reading; actually it shows the intense interest with which people in the west followed the time made by the Pony Express riders.)

The weather has been very disagreeable and stormy for the past week and in every way calculated to retard the operations of the company, and we are informed that the Express eastward was five hours in going from this place to Snyder's Mill, a distance of 25 miles.

The probability is that the Express will be a little behind time in reaching Sacramento this trip, but when the weather becomes settled and the roads good, we have no doubt that they will be able to make the trip in less than ten days.

The first run from St. Joseph to Sacramento took nine days and twenty-three hours, one hour ahead of schedule. The first eastbound run took exactly ten days. On the other hand, the Butterfield stage took twenty-five days on the southern route. The Express had cut the time for the delivery of mail by more than half.

As there was now a telegraph line between San Francisco and Carson City in Nevada, important messages could be sent quite rapidly from coast to coast. For example, a message could be telegraphed from say New York or Washington to St. Joseph. From St. Joseph it proceeded by Pony Express to Carson City. Here it was telegraphed to San Francisco. Californians were overjoyed at this vast improvement in service.

More letters were sent from California than to it. About 350 letters left California for the East on each trip. Much of the Pony Express mail went to senators and congressmen in Washington. Some of it was destined for the War Department. A few were addressed to the President and doubtless contained words of encouragement or promises of support.

Many of the letters were from western businessmen to commercial firms in the large cities of the East. Thus, the Pony Express played an important role in stimulating business. One of the most interesting uses of the Pony Express was the shipping of British diplomatic documents from Asiatic countries to the Pacific coast and thence, by Pony Express, to Missouri. Eventually, this mail arrived in London after going to New York and then being forwarded across the Atlantic. This represented a very valuable saving of time as opposed to the previous shipping of documents and messages all the way by ocean—a matter of many weeks.

When the Pony Express started, the rate for carrying mail was five dollars per half-ounce letter. This was later reduced to one dollar an ounce. Even so, some letters sent by commercial firms cost as much as twenty-five dollars—but apparently they were well worth it.

The Pony Express had quickly proved its value. But its troubles were only beginning.

6 *A Home Away from Home*

THE SUCCESS of the Pony Express depended on its ability to establish relay stations, especially in the outlying territories. The opportunity to replace exhausted animals with fresh, rested mounts was absolutely essential to the enterprise.

In fairly well-settled regions, it was easy to establish stations on existing facilities, and on a fairly inexpensive basis. But as the trail went west and became more rugged in sparsely settled country, serious problems arose. There, stations had to be built from scratch, with at least two men to operate them. In addition to the cabin, a stable and corral had to be built. Horsethieves —red or white—had to be guarded against constantly.

The most dangerous locality was in western Utah and eastern Nevada. Here were the home grounds of the Paiutes, the most hostile Indians of all. Despite the real dangers involved, these exposed stations never lacked brave men who were willing to serve as station keepers.

The locations of the stations were based on the distance that rider and horse could normally cover without exhaustion. Because of this requirement a station was not always placed safely or conveniently. Sometimes, for example, this meant that grass and water were not handy. In that case it was necessary to bring back water in barrels and to drive the horses some distance away to feed them.

As a rule the home stations had already been set up

earlier as stagecoach stations. The worst of the stations had the most rudimentary accommodations, with dirt floors and no glass windows. Bunks were built into the walls in place of beds, and the furniture was limited to boxes and benches.

The stations required a large variety of supplies. Foods included hams, bacon, flour, syrup, dried fruits, corn meal. Tea and coffee were the standard beverages, but no form of alcoholic drink was permitted.

There was an almost bewildering assortment of housekeeping materials, such as axes, hammers, saws, stoves, brooms, tin dishes, both tin and wooden buckets, candles, blankets, matches, scissors, needles, and thread.

The equipment for the stable included bridles, rope, and blacksmith's supplies; brushes, currycombs, and manure forks. In the way of medicines, the stations had borax, castor oil, cream of tartar, and turpentine on hand. Among the other things we might mention are: screws, hinges, putty, wagon grease, twine, safes, buffalo robes, and antelope skins.

Home stations—where a rider finished his run— needed a more elaborate set-up. They had to provide facilities for the riders and they also took care of such services as blacksmithing. The men who did this work had to be top-notch in their field, for many of the horses were half wild and needed to be held down while the blacksmith got through with his trying and often dangerous work. Even so, shoeing might take half of a working day.

So harried was the life of a Pony Express rider that he rarely got to know the station tender really well. There was no time for that—just a quick rush in and out, with perhaps a quick word of warning or valuable advice. Even acquaintanceship between riders was rare, for theirs was a lonely assignment which did not bring them into contact with other riders. This was even true of home stations, where a rider's chief ambition was to catch up on badly needed sleep.

When time approached for the arrival of a Pony Express rider at a station, the keeper had a fresh horse saddled and bridled well in advance. In the daytime a large cloud of dust gave notice of his arrival. The clear air in the mountains often gave the station keeper a chance to see the approaching rider from quite a distance if there were no obstructions.

At first, the riders had a horn to announce their arrival. But these horns were discarded in the effort to carry as little weight as possible. As a matter of fact the sounds of the horse's hoofbeats was as good a signal of arrival as any. As he approached, the rider would loosen his *mochila* so that he could toss it to the keeper at the earliest possible moment.

The men at the station sometimes worked under great tension and did not always get on too well together. This account from the *Carson City Territorial Enterprise* tells its own story:

One day last week, H. Trumbo, station keeper at Smith's Creek, got into a difficulty with Montgomery Maze, one of the Pony Express riders, during which Trumbo snapped a pistol at Maze several times. The next day the fracas was renewed, when Maze shot Trumbo with a rifle, the ball entering a little above the hip and inflicting a dangerous wound. Maze has since arrived at this place, bringing with him a certificate signed by various parties, exonerating him from blame in the affair and setting forth that Trumbo had provoked the attack.

Some of the stations were rugged beyond belief. This is how Burton described the station at Dugway: "A hole, four feet deep, roofed over with split cedar trunks and with a rough adobe chimney. Water had to be brought in casks. We had to skirt an alkali slough to the next station."

As for food, Burton notes: "Diet is sometimes reduced to 'wolf mutton' or a little boiled wheat or rye; their drink is brackish water." Even with such conditions prevailing, the station-keepers shared their meager food supply with the Indians, sometimes to win their friendship, sometimes just out of simple kindness. Here is an instance quoted by the *Deseret News* of Salt Lake City:

A person in the service of the Mail and Express Company, situated on the route between this city and Carson, was in our office a few days since, and reported that the snow was very deep in places along the route; that the weather had been very cold, and that the Indians, particularly in the vicinity of Roberts Creek station were in a destitute and starving condition. One Indian was recently found dead within a half mile of the station, who had perished of cold and starvation while on his way there for food. Another had fallen down nearby from exhaustion, badly frozen, who was seen, taken to the station and resuscitated before it was too late to save his life.

It is not surprising that the Indians, in their need, would steal horses, food, blankets, or clothing if given the opportunity. This was one of the many trials endured by the station keepers, a heroic breed to whom history has not done justice because they lacked the glamor of the Pony Express riders.

7 *Indians on the Warpath*

THE FIRST AMERICANS who came to the West were the trappers—the "mountain men." They cultivated the Indians' good will because they wanted to trade with them. The Indians supplied valuable furs, and in return received guns, blankets, household goods, cheap trinkets and—unfortunately—whisky. There were few trappers, and they had no permanent residence and no families. The Indians' way of life and food supply remained undisturbed. The trappers often adopted Indian customs and sometimes married Indian girls. Friendships between white men and Indians were quite common; a state of mutual trust was the general rule.

But by the time the 1840s came to an end, the fur trade had dwindled considerably. Then, with the discovery of gold, large numbers of white men began swarming over the trails into the Far West. This meant disaster for the Indians, who saw their timber being chopped down, their game disappearing. As their resentment grew, attacks and ambushes multiplied. The white men replied in kind, directing their anger at the innocent as well as the guilty.

The feeling of mutual hostility was further intensified by the white man's continual breaking of treaties which had been solemnly entered into by the Indians and the United States Government. Very often the government agents, who had been appointed to take care of the

74

PONY EXPRESS HISTORY AND ART GALLERY

This building on the outskirts of Hanover, Kansas, is the only remaining unaltered Pony Express station.

A Pony Express rider, en route to San Francisco, is pursued by Indians.

Indians' interests, actually did the opposite. Time and again the Indians were fleeced and driven from their homes and hunting grounds as the white man broke his promises once more.

What troubled the Indians perhaps more than anything else was the white man's systematic and seemingly senseless slaughter of the buffalo. To the Indian this animal was a source not only of food but also of clothing, shelter, utensils, weapons.

In Utah and Nevada there were no buffalo, but the Paiute Indians who lived there had been uneasy about the white man's arrival from the very start. Their chief stand-by in the way of food was antelope, and they also relied on nuts gathered from the piñon trees. Life was hard in this bleak country of canyon and desert.

At first, the Paiutes viewed the coming of the Mormons with hostility. But when they attacked the Mormon wagon trains they soon found out that arrows were no match for bullets. So the Paiutes confined themselves to killing lone travelers and stealing horses and cattle.

Eventually the Mormons and Indians learned to live together in reasonably friendly fashion. The Mormons made it clear that they were looking for new homes and had no intention of monopolizing the land. They showed respect for Indian customs and Indian hunting rights, which they scrupulously honored.

But a few years after peace had been established, the Forty-Niners started their trek westward. They shot first and asked questions afterwards. The hostility between the two races again flared. But this passed in time.

With the coming of the stagecoach lines, stations were established along the routes. The station keepers were experienced in the ways of Indians and knew how to get along with them. Once more an uneasy truce prevailed.

The coming of the Pony Express introduced an element of uncertainty once more. Some tribes, such as the Shoshones, the Kickapoos and the Pawnees, were consistently friendly. The Paiutes were inclined to be hostile, while the Cheyennes and the Crows were unknown quantities. There was no knowing in advance whether a party of them would be friendly or hostile. And unfortunately, the lone Pony Express riders made inviting targets.

Pony Express riders had been instructed never to provoke the Indians and never to shoot first. Their horses were swifter than those of the Indians, and the Pony Express had the best riders. Swift flight was safest —it saved lives and it saved time as well. Still, after a few weeks, reports of Indian attacks began to trickle in. The attack on a single rider was tempting, and the mysterious mail boxes intrigued the savages.

It speaks well for the fortitude and the skill of the Pony Express riders that during the whole time the Pony Express was in existence only one mail was lost with a rider. In one case the horseman was killed, but his riderless mount galloped in with the mail. Yet so pervasive was the danger, that a San Francisco paper claimed that the Pony Express was "simply inviting slaughter on all the foolhardy young men engaged as riders." Perhaps that sentiment was hardheaded and realistic, but the Pony Express riders were a superior breed.

In May, 1860, the Paiutes finally went on the warpath, nearly eight thousand strong. Most of them still used the powerful war bow, but many had rifles by this time. No part of Nevada was safe from them. Soon they were joined by the Shoshones in California, who were angered by the wanton killing of an old tribesman.

Though the Pony Express riders were completely innocent of any outrages against the Indians, they were now considered fair game over an area of thousands of square miles. The way stations, those isolated outposts, were equally vulnerable. One raid after another hit the stations. The Indians would kill every man they found, and then would burn down the cabins after taking away the horses and removing whatever supplies they found.

The strain on the Pony Express riders became almost unbearable, especially since a weary courier, after completing a bone-breaking ride, would then have to keep riding because his replacement had been wounded or because no fresh horses were available.

Nick Wilson was a Pony Express rider who was wounded so badly that he was given up for dead; and yet he lived to tell the tale. This is how it happened:

Arriving at the Spring Valley relay station, he was surprised to find that the keeper was not there. However, the station was intact, and some relay horses were grazing near the cabins. So Nick jumped off his horse, removed the saddle, and started on his way to the stable to get a fresh horse. Suddenly a bloodcurdling war whoop rang out. Nick turned in time to see two Indians leading the relay horses away.

Instead of thinking of his own safety, Nick pulled out his Colt and started firing at the Indians. But they were already out of range. Impulsively he ran after them, following them into a cedar grove. Suddenly another Indian jumped out from behind a tree, drawing his bow at Nick.

It was too late to dodge. The stone-tipped arrow hit the boy above the left eye and more than half the arrowhead penetrated his skull. He lay among the cedars, unconscious. But now his luck turned. A few hours later, two young men who had been making their way out of the desert happened to find him.

In trying to pull out the arrow they loosened the shaft from the stone tip, leaving it more firmly imbedded than ever. Although it seemed to them that Nick was near death, they gently moved him into the shade, and made off as rapidly as they could to get help at the next relay station.

The following morning, two Pony Express men came out to the grove to bury the dead rider. However, they found Nick still alive, although he had not regained consciousness. They tied him firmly across a saddle and set out to bring him back to the Ruby Valley Station, though they doubted that he would survive the trip.

But Nick managed to fool them. He did last out the trip, and he responded to good medical care. A skillful doctor successfully removed the arrowhead. Though Nick remained unconscious for several days, he eventually recovered, and several weeks later he was again riding for the Pony Express. For the rest of his long life, however, Nick Wilson always wore a hat cocked over his left eye to conceal the ugly hole made by the stone arrowhead.

Bob Haslam, one of the most famous of the Pony Express riders, also had some exciting experiences during this period. One night he rode into the Dry Creek Station, only to find that the whole staff had been murdered. Further on, the Cold Springs Station had been burned down, with the dead body of the keeper left lying in the ashes. Going on to the Sand Creek Station, he prevailed on the keeper to leave with him. That night the station was destroyed.

Another time Pony Bob galloped into an ambush of thirty Paiutes. Calmly, he drew out his revolver as he approached them. At the last moment the leader let him pass unharmed, perhaps out of admiration for his daring.

Narrow escapes from a cruel death were not infrequent. At the Egan Canyon Station, Henry Wilson and Albert Armstrong were quietly eating their breakfast one morning, when they suddenly found themselves surrounded by a war party of Indians. Quickly snatching up their rifles, Wilson and Armstrong killed or wounded several of the attackers before they were overcome by sheer force of numbers.

Their captors tied them up and piled brush and firewood around them, intending to burn them alive in the cabin. But fortunately, the Indians had not had their breakfast. They ate all the food in sight and went rummaging for more.

Suddenly, the welcome sound of hoofbeats was heard. The captives cried desperately for help. They were lucky. A band of soldiers from a nearby post was on patrol. They opened fire on the Indians, eighteen of whom were killed. The rest ran for their ponies and quickly made off.

But the luck of the Pony Express riders could not be expected to hold out forever. Alexander Majors announced that unless military protection was forthcoming, he could no longer allow his riders to risk their lives. He was as good as his word; on May 31, 1860, he stopped all service.

No more fast mail delivery was available. At once there was an outcry from the people of the Far West, where the pioneers, after ten years of dreary isolation, had been getting news and letters in wonderfully quick time.

One newspaper after another kept calling on the government to send some troops to the threatened area to keep the Indians in check. Typical of these newspapers was the *St. Louis Globe-Democrat*'s reaction:

> The Pony Express is already assuming great importance to California, and large amounts of original drafts are now forwarded by this conveyance. A considerable amount was received in St. Louis by the last arrival, and as the usefulness of this quick communication becomes more and more apparent, these valuable trusts will increase.
>
> It is a matter, therefore, of the highest importance that the bold and daring spirits who risk their necks in carrying a sack of letters through the defiles of the mountains, over unbroken prairies and through the rapid rivers which divide us from the Pacific, should be protected. If these gallant fellows cannot perform their circuit unmolested, the Express will have to be abandoned, and the whole country affected thereby. It is bad enough that our government compels the public to rely on private enterprise for this service, when a liberal encouragement in the form of a mail contract should be extended. But to refuse protection afforded by the presence of troops already near the ground would be infamous.

A force of one hundred five men under a Major Ormsby set out from Carson City, Nevada to bring the

Paiutes to their senses. Unfortunately, Major Ormsby, and apparently the men under him as well, had had no experience in Indian fighting. Taking no precautions against a sudden attack, they were ambushed so effectively that the major and nearly half of his men were butchered. The rest beat a quick retreat back to Carson City.

Later, one of the Indians commented: "White men all cry a heap; got no gun, throw 'um away; got no revolver, throw 'um away too; no want to fight any more now; all big scare, just like cattle, run, run, cry, cry, heap cry, same as papoose; no want Injun to kill 'um any more."

Now even the regular stagecoach service was in danger. To meet this critical situation the government finally dispatched a force of regular army troops who harried the Indians back into the mountains and beat them badly during a snowstorm (in June!). However, sporadic raids still took place, for no army could keep such a vast area under complete control.

Three weeks passed without any Pony Express service. This was serious, not only for the settlers, but for the firm of Russell, Majors & Waddell. For the firm's hope of getting a proper subsidy from Congress depended on its furnishing regular, dependable service. But mail delivery had been interrupted, and thus the company's claim to a subsidy from the government no longer had adequate grounds.

Nor was this the only blow to the company. Many of its riders, after coping with danger and privation with the utmost bravery, came to feel that it would be senseless to continue exposing themselves to Indian attacks in which they were hopelessly outnumbered. More and more riders were leaving the company's employ.

But Russell was far from ready to call it quits. New stock and equipment were provided for stations that had been attacked. New riders were hired, and on June 26, the Pony Express resumed operations. The mails were being moved again.

The Indian outrages lost the company $75,000. But Russell, Majors, and Waddell showed their confidence by increasing service from weekly to semi-weekly. The newspapers backed them: until telegraph wires spanned the continent, the Express was the best they had.

Not all the Pony Express riders were content to react passively to Indian depredations. Years later, Buffalo Bill, then a young rider named Billy Cody, recalled with relish an entertaining punitive expedition against the Indians:

The Indians had now become so bad and had stolen so much stock that it was decided to stop the Pony Express for at least six weeks, and to run the stages only occasionally during that period; in fact, it would have been impossible to continue that enterprise much longer without restocking the line.

While we were thus lying idle, a party was organized to go out and search for stolen stock. This party was composed of stage drivers, express riders, stock tenders and ranchmen—forty of them altogether—and they were well armed and well mounted. They were mostly men who had undergone all kinds of hardships and braved every danger, and they were ready and anxious to tackle any number of Indians.

Wild Bill, who had been driving stage on the road and had recently come down to our division, was elected captain of the company. It was supposed that the stolen stock had been taken to the head of the Powder River and vicinity, and the party, of which I was a member, started out for that section in high hopes of success.

There is an interesting psychological point here. When these men, in their capacity as riders, drivers, etc., were on the defensive against the Indians, they were naturally very discouraged. As soon as they were able to take the offensive, however, their mood brightened perceptibly.

Twenty miles out from Sweetwater Bridge, at the head of Horse Creek, we found an Indian trail running north toward Powder River, and we could see by the tracks that most of the horses had been recently shod and were undoubtedly our stolen stage stock. Pushing rapidly forward, we followed this trail to Powder River; thence down this stream to within about forty miles of the spot where old Fort Reno now stands.

Here the trail took a more westerly course along the foot of the mountains, leading eventually to Crazy Woman's Fork—a tributary of Powder River. At this point we discovered that the party whom we were trailing had been joined by another band of Indians, and judging from the fresh appearance of the trail, the united body could not have left this spot more than twenty-four hours before.

Being aware that we were now in the heart of the hostile country and might at any moment find more Indians than we had lost, we advanced with more caution than usual and kept a sharp lookout. As we were approaching Clear Creek, another tributary of

Powder River, we discovered Indians on the opposite side of the creek, some three miles distant; at least we saw horses grazing, which was a sure sign that there were Indians there.

The Indians, thinking themselves in comparative safety, never before having been followed so far into their own country by white men, had neglected to put out any scouts. They had no idea that there were any white men in that part of the country. We got the lay of their camp, and then held a council to consider and mature a plan for capturing it.

We knew full well that the Indians would out-number us at least three to one, and perhaps more. Upon the advice and suggestion of Wild Bill, it was finally decided that we should wait until it was nearly dark, and then after creeping as close to them as pos-sible, make a dash through their camp, open a gen-eral fire on them, and then stampede the horses.

This plan, at the proper time, was very successfully executed. The dash upon the enemy was a complete surprise to them. They were so overcome with aston-ishment that they did not know what to make of it. We could not have astounded them any more had we dropped down into their camp from the clouds. They did not recover from the surprise of this sudden charge until after we had ridden pell-mell through their camp and got away with our own horses as well as theirs.

We at once circled the horses around toward the south, and after getting them on the south side of Clear Creek, some twenty of our men, just as the darkness was coming on, rode back and gave the In-dians a few parting shots. We then took up our line of march for Sweetwater Bridge, where we arrived four days afterwards with all our own horses and about one hundred captured Indian ponies.

But Indians were not the only danger on the lonely trails to California. Pony Express riders and stagecoach drivers also had to contend with white enemies—the outlaws. In some cases they were habitual criminals who had left the East for more profitable territories. Some were dishonest gamblers who had become too well known to be able to ply their trade in their former haunts. Sometimes, miners who had failed in their hope of finding gold became professional "bad men." Generally working in pairs, they would occasionally form larger bands.

While stagecoaches were favored as providing the more profitable booty, Pony Express riders were sometimes attacked on the chance that the mail would provide some good prizes. One of the Pony Express riders at this time was a thin, wiry youngster who was not quite seventeen. He was a good shot and a fine horseman.

On one of his trips he was assigned to carry a box of money in addition to the regular mail. There had been reports that two outlaws were operating in the area, so the young man decided to be careful. He hid his *mochila* and mail cases by covering them with a second leather blanket to which four *cantinas* were fastened. They looked like the real thing, but they were actually filled with worthless papers.

As he was riding through a narrow defile, he was stopped by two men who ordered him to dismount and put his hands up. After he got off the horse, one of the men reached out for the blanket. Quick as lightning, the boy flung the blanket in his face, pulled out his gun and shot him. Leaping back on his horse, he rode down the other bandit and made good his escape. The youthful rider was William F. Cody who later became world-famous as "Buffalo Bill."

Julesburg was a rough frontier town in Colorado, near Fort Kearny. An important station of the overland stagecoach route was located here. Jules Reni, a French Canadian frontiersman who was division agent for the Pony Express, was also in charge of the station. Jules was a heavy drinker, a powerfully built man, utterly unscrupulous, and a bully.

In those days, Julesburg was a gathering place for unsavory characters and for soldiers, traders, hunters, and other frontiersmen who went there to spend their money on riotous pleasure. Strange things were happening in this area. The stage schedules were disordered. Wagon trains were attacked by outlaws. Livestock was stolen. Somewhere, somehow, the thieves were getting the information they needed to bring off their robberies. They were appearing too often in the right place and at the right time to carry out their hold-ups.

Soon the suspicion gained ground that Jules was the leader of the outlaws and the source of their uncannily accurate information. Eventually Russell, Majors, and Waddell discharged Jules and replaced him with a man named Slade.

Slade was something of a man of mystery. He had fought in the Mexican War and insisted on being addressed as Captain Slade. Though he had been involved in some fatal shootings, his courteous manners gave him a deceptive appearance of softness.

Furious at his discharge and replacement, Jules ambushed Slade and shot him in cold blood. The wounds were not fatal, and during his recovery, Slade swore that he would kill Jules and wear his ears on his watch chain. Jules for his part swore that he would kill Slade in their next encounter.

In the end Slade took a terrible revenge. He rounded up a posse, trapped Jules, and took him prisoner. Then, instead of turning over his enemy for trial, he tied him to a post and shot him repeatedly until he finally finished him off. This brutal killing was something that Slade never lived down; it gave people an insight into his true character.

Not that Slade wanted to live down his reputation. He was absolutely ferocious in ferreting out and punishing outlaws and other wrongdoers, and in the process he became more and more ruthless.

In *Roughing It* Mark Twain describes his surprise on meeting Slade:

He was so friendly and gentle-spoken that I warmed to him in spite of his awful history. It was hardly possible to realize that this pleasant person was the pitiless scourge of the outlaws, the raw-head-and-bloody-bones the nursing mothers of the mountains terrified their children with. And to this day I can remember nothing remarkable about Slade except that his face was rather broad across the cheek-bones, and that the cheek-bones were low and the lips peculiarly thin and straight. But that was enough to leave something of an effect on me, for since then I seldom see a face possessing those characteristics without fancying that the owner is a dangerous man.

Slade was indeed dangerous—dangerous even to himself. Eventually, he came to a bad end which made a rather ironic sequel to his law-enforcement career. After engaging in some minor destruction during a drinking spree he was discharged by the Overland Mail. He went out to a mining camp in Virginia City, Montana, where he publicly threatened a judge. This happened at a time when a vigilante committee was over-zealously restoring law and order to the region. His threats, led to his public hanging by the vigilantes.

8 *"The Mail Must Go Through!"*

"BART RILES, the pony rider, died this morning from wounds received at Cold Springs, May 16."

"The men at Dry Creek Station have all been killed, and it is thought that those at Robert's Creek have met with the same fate."

"Six Pike's Peakers found the body of the station keeper horribly mutilated, the station burned, and all the stock missing from Simpson's."

"Eight horses were stolen from Smith's Creek on last Monday, supposedly by road agents [outlaws]."

Newspaper items like these tell us very simply of the dangers to which the Pony Express riders and station keepers were exposed. It took cool courage and resourcefulness to come through such dangers successfully. Many are the stories of memorable rides, of loyalty and devotion, of hair's-breadth escapes, of quick thinking and incredible endurance.

J. G. Kelley worked with Superintendent Bolivar Roberts in laying out the Pony Express route across Nevada. One of the most difficult sections was along the Carson River, where it was necessary to build a corduroy road made of tree trunks. After cutting down nearby willow trees, the men cut the trunks into the proper lengths and then carried them in their arms for three hundred yards, plagued all the way by large swarms of mosquitoes.

At the sink of the Carson, so called because the river

bed was much lower at that point, Kelley helped construct a fort as protection against the Indians. As the area was bare of bricks or timber, the men had to use adobe mud which they got to the right consistency by tramping it all day. Because the soil was heavily alkaline their feet swelled up horribly.

Later on, Kelley was appointed assistant station keeper at Cold Springs. This was at the time the Paiute Indians were on the warpath.

One night when Kelley was on guard duty, he noticed that the horses were very restive. Peering around watchfully, Kelley saw an Indian at the outer wall. He shot at him but missed. The Indian ran away. Next morning many tracks were found outside the stockade. Kelley's vigilance had saved the station and its crew.

That morning Bart Riles, a young Mexican Pony Express rider, managed to reach the station although he had been fatally wounded in an ambush at nearby Quaking Aspen Bottom. Someone had to replace the dead boy to deliver the mail, and Kelley was chosen.

After completing his mission he turned back toward the station. Soon he came to the thicket where Bart had been mortally wounded. This was perhaps the most dangerous part of the whole trail, as the road zigzagged constantly on a path so narrow that only one horse could pass at a time. On this two-mile stretch it was impossible to see more than forty feet ahead at any point—an ideal spot for an ambush.

Kelley was on the alert. He got out his repeating rifle and galloped through as fast as he could. He got past safely and then stopped at the top of a hill when he saw some bushes moving. Quickly he fired into the underbrush and the movement stopped. He returned to the station safely. A few days later two soldiers were trapped in this same thicket and murdered.

On one occasion when Kelley was delivering mail he galloped past a wagon train. Suddenly, without any warning, a whole broadside of bullets flew past him. Though he was seething with rage, Kelley's first thought was of the mail, and he made off to the next station.

However, on his return trip he met the emigrants and reproached them in salty language for their wild attack. Abashed, they replied: "We thought you was an Injun!" Such incidents were not uncommon, for the Pony Express riders were so deeply tanned from exposure to the sun that they could easily be mistaken for Indians. And, as we have seen, it was the emigrants' custom to shoot first, and look or explain afterwards.

By July, 1860, the Indian troubles had quieted down considerably. The ranks of the Pony Express had been filled up again to replace the riders who had dropped out.

By this time there were almost two hundred stations, some as little as ten miles apart, none more than twenty. As a rule, riders covered about eight miles an hour, and about two hundred miles a week. Clearly this was a very taxing schedule, even under the best of circumstances.

But the circumstances were not always of the best. There was the time, for example, when Pony Bob Haslam made a seventy-five mile ride to the Reese River Station, where he expected to change horses. This was at the height of the Paiute War, and when he arrived at the station he found that all the horses had been requisitioned for Indian fighting.

Though his mount was exhausted, Pony Bob had no

choice. He got back on the weary animal and set out for Buckland's, fifteen miles away. But when he arrived, he found that the rider who was scheduled to replace him refused to do so. With so many Indian war parties on the prowl, he evidently felt that discretion was the better part of valor.

No one else was available to carry the mail, so Pony Bob, bone-weary as he was, had to start out on a new run. At least he had a fresh mount for this trip. Before he was through he had passed three more stations—an additional hundred miles, or 190 miles in all of almost continuous riding!

But he was still not finished. The rider from the opposite direction had been so badly hurt in a fall that he was in no condition for riding. So after an hour and a half of deep sleep, Pony Bob was roused to make the return trip. He started to retrace the route he had taken previously. At the Cold Springs Station, which he had left a few hours earlier, he found that all five men of the crew had been murdered by the Indians, and all the horses had been stolen.

When he arrived at Buckland's he was ordered to wait for nightfall before going on, as there would be less danger from the Indians. At least this gave him an opportunity for nine hours of precious sleep. Then Pony Bob continued on his weary way to the next station, though he was in constant danger of being trapped by Indians. Once a party of Indians sighted him, but he was too quick for them and escaped to safety. Finally, after 380 miles he was back at his starting point. And despite all his hardships, he had lost less than four hours of the scheduled time.

For this remarkable feat the company presented him with a special hundred-dollar prize.

It goes without saying that the horses used on such rides had to be spirited, mettlesome creatures. Later, Levi Hensel recalled his experiences as a blacksmith:

> I had the contract to shoe the Overland stage and Pony Express horses that ran from Kennekuk to Big Sandy up to the time that I threw down my hammer and went into the army. Sometimes they ran ponies in from Fort Kearny and beyond to be shod.
>
> The animals that John Frey and Jim Beatley used to ride were the worst imps of Satan in the business. The only way that I could master them was to throw them and get a rope around each foot, stake them out, and have a man on the head and another on the body, while I trimmed the hoofs and nailed down the shoes. They would squeal and bite all the time I was working with them. It generally took half a day to shoe one of them. But travel! They never seemed to get tired.

Henry Avis performed a singular act of heroism for which he received a special bonus of three hundred dollars. His run went through a region in which many hostile Sioux Indians were found.

On one of his trips Henry finished his run at Horseshoe Station, the western end of his route. The rider who was to replace him for the westward trip to Deer Creek Station refused to do so when it was reported that a party of Sioux was on the warpath in the area.

Arriving at Deer Creek safely, Henry found that the station had been burned and all the horses stolen. Now it was the eastward-bound rider who refused to take the mail. So Henry fastened the *mochila* on again and turned back to Horseshoe Station. Again he made the trip safely, after completing 220 miles of hard riding. His daring was well rewarded by the handsome bonus.

Howard Ransom Egan also had a remarkable adventure when he replaced a sick comrade. Riding through Egan Canyon in the dark, he caught the gleam of a camp fire. On approaching it cautiously, he discovered an Indian war party.

His first impulse was to gallop off. But he reasoned that another war party was at the other end of the canyon waiting to trap him. Thereupon, he came to a bold decision. Spurring on his horse, he galloped into the camp with deafening shouts and fired his revolver into the air. The startled Indians, fearing an attack by a large group of white men, scuttled off without a second look. He then took a short cut and arrived safely. The next day he learned that just as he had suspected, another Indian war party had been waiting to ambush him.

William Frederick Fisher had at least one narrow escape from death. In January, 1861, he set out on his run from Rush Valley to Salt Lake City. Soon a thick snowfall started, but he managed to find his way to Camp Floyd. There he was advised to take shelter until the storm abated. His only reply was, "The mail must go through."

Before long he found himself lost in the hills. Unable to get his bearings, he dismounted and sheltered himself as best he could behind his horse. He found it impossible to stay awake, but just as he was falling asleep a jackrabbit jumped on his legs.

This woke him up. Realizing his danger, he thrashed

his arms about and stamped upon the snow until he felt fully awake and less cold. Then he got on his horse, tied the reins together, gripped the saddle horn firmly and let his horse go on undirected. An hour of aimless wandering followed until he finally got his bearings. Soon he came to Lehi, a small town on his route. Here he was fed and given a chance to get warm.

As soon as he could he got back on his horse and went on in the direction of Salt Lake City. After several hours he realized that he was again lost, this time in a deeply snowed-in ravine. In this predicament he had the good luck to see a light from a nearby ranch house.

Dismounting, he struggled through the snow to the dwelling. Here he was given a kindly welcome and one of the men went out and brought his horse to shelter.

After warming himself, eating, and resting, he again went resolutely on his way, arriving in Salt Lake City shortly before dawn. The whole trip had been filled with the kind of hardship that the Pony Express riders took for granted.

Johnny Frey was one of the outstanding Pony Express riders. His run was between St. Joseph and Seneca, Kansas. Legend has it that Johnny was a great favorite with the girls, who would wait for him on the trail to give him cakes, cookies, and other delicacies. This was a great treat for Johnny, as the riders had very little time for eating and their food was of the plainest. He would grab the girls' offerings on the run, reaching out one hand while keeping the other on the reins. Then he would gulp down the food as he rode away.

It is said that the girls, seeing how awkward it was for Johnny to grasp the food, hit on the idea of making cookies with a hole in the middle, so that Johnny could simply stick a finger through the hole as he passed by. According to one theory, this is how the doughnut originated. If this is not true, it is certainly a good story.

An equally delightful story tells of a young seamstress who was making a "Log Cabin" quilt. She was eager to sew into this quilt a gaudy red tie of which Johnny was very fond. One day, knowing that he would be coming along soon, she got on her horse and made her way to the trail.

When Johnny appeared, she rode alongside him and asked for the tie; but, as she had anticipated, he again refused to part with it. He galloped off, but she caught up with him and reached out for the tie. But she missed, and instead grabbed hold of his shirt tail. A part of the shirt tail tore off, and this is what she sewed into the quilt.

There is also a delightful story about Thomas Owen King, who had a run between Salt Lake City and Fort Bridger. One night, as he was changing horses at Bear River Station, he told the keeper that he hadn't met Henry Worley, who was supposed to be riding on the same trail, but in the opposite direction. Meanwhile Worley, when he arrived at his station that night, reported that he hadn't met King.

What had happened, of course, was that both riders were so weary that they had passed each other in the night, fast asleep on their horses. These animals knew the trails so well that they had no trouble covering the route without any guidance from their riders.

Billy Cody, before he became famous as Buffalo Bill, carried messages for Russell, Majors & Waddell's freight-wagon trains when he was fourteen. Later on, he was hired by the Kansas Pacific Railroad to obtain buffalo meat to feed its construction crews. His daily quota was twelve buffalo. It was from his extensive slaughter of these animals that he was given the nickname "Buffalo Bill."

On one occasion he and Billy Comstock, another notable shot, competed to see who could kill the most buffalo in a single day. One of the railroads ran a special train from St. Louis so that spectators could see the "fun." Buffalo Bill won convincingly by a score of sixty-nine kills to forty-six.

After his buffalo-killing chore was completed, Cody became a scout for the army in the Indian wars. He had many thrilling adventures but finally left the army and settled down for a while near North Platte, Nebraska, where he became a Justice of the Peace. It is said that when he performed his first marriage ceremony he concluded it with these words: "Whoever God and Buffalo Bill have joined together let no man put asunder. Two dollars please."

On a trip east Cody met a picturesque rogue named Ned Buntline who had made money in a number of ways, including the writing of enormously popular dime novels. Buntline persuaded Cody to go on the stage with a crony named "Texas Jack." Their lively re-enactment of their western adventures drew packed audiences.

Later on, when a punitive expedition was organized against the Sioux in retaliation for the Custer massacre, Cody took part. Many stories, legends, and lies have been woven around his famous hand-to-hand duel with Yellow Hand, the Indian chieftain.

After this interlude Buffalo Bill invented the Wild West show, complete with cowboys, Indians, buffalo, and stagecoaches. This uproarious spectacle was enormously successful when Cody toured with it all over the country and in Europe. Despite this success he became enmeshed in financial troubles and later performed in circuses up to the age of seventy-one. He then retired and died the following year.

At the height of his fame Cody turned up as the hero of Colonel Prentiss Ingraham's sensationally best-selling dime novel, *The Pony Express Rider; or Buffalo Bill's Frontier Feats*. Colonel Ingraham owed his fantastic success to the simple stratagem of capitalizing on Buffalo Bill's fame by inventing a mythical but realistic past in which the youth performed all kinds of heroic deeds fashioned from the whole cloth, interwoven here and there with little bits of truth.

To pour on additional glamour Colonel Ingraham had the young Billy Cody share some adventures with Wild Bill Hickok, another famous frontier fighter for whom the Colonel invented equally exciting and equally mythical adventures. Here is a sample of Billy Cody's derring-do as fabricated by the Colonel:

One day as he sped along like the wind he saw ahead of him the stagecoach going at full speed and no one in the box.

At once he knew there was trouble, and as he drew nearer he discovered some Indians dash out of a ravine and give chase.

As he heard the clatter of hoofs behind him he looked around and saw a dozen redskins in pursuit.

The stagecoach was now in the open prairie, and dashing along the trail as fast as the horses could go, while the Indians in close pursuit numbered but three.

Billy was well mounted upon a sorrel mare, and urging her with the spur he soon came in range of the redskin furthest in the rear and hastily fired.

Down went the pony, and the Indian was thrown with such violence that he was evidently stunned, as he lay where he had fallen.

Another shot wounded one of the remaining Indians, and they hastily sped away to the right oblique in flight, while Billy dashed on to the side of the coach.

There were five passengers within, and two of them were women, and all were terribly frightened, though evidently not knowing that their driver lay dead upon the box, the reins still grasped in his nerveless hands.

Riding near, Billy seized his mail bags and dextrously got from his saddle to the stage, and the next instant he held the reins in his firm grip.

He knew well that Ted Remus, the driver, had carried out a box of gold, and was determined to save it for the company if in his power.

His horse, relieved of his weight and trained to run the trail, kept right on ahead, and he, skillfully handling the reins, for he was a fine driver, drove on at the topmost speed of the six animals drawing the coach.

Behind him came the Indians, steadily gaining; but Billy plied the silk in a style that made his team fly, and they soon reached the hills.

Here the redskins again gained, for the road was not good and in many places very dangerous.

But once over the ridge, and just as the Indians were near enough to fill the back of the coach with arrows, Billy made his team jump ahead once more, and at breakneck speed they rushed down the steep road, the vehicle swaying wildly, and the passengers within not knowing whether they would be dashed to pieces, or scalped by the Indians, or which death would be the most desired. But Billy, in spite of his lightning driving, managed his team well, and after a fierce run of half an hour rolled up to the door of the station in a style that made the agent and the lookers-on stare.

Nineteenth-century readers loved it. Today these dime-novel feats have been moved to the television medium.

9 California and the Civil War

IN THE CLOSING MONTHS of 1860, the Pony Express took on even added importance. The hostility between North and South had become so intense that the South threatened to secede if Abraham Lincoln, the Republican candidate, was elected.

In this tense atmosphere, heavy with foreboding of the conflict to come, both North and South were speculating on what role California would play. That far-off, isolated state was still shipping vast quantities of gold to the East. In case a civil war broke out, this gold would be of prime importance in buying ammunition and supplies in foreign countries.

The possibility of seizing control of California had many attractions for the South. The most obvious prize was of course the gold supply, an important consideration for a cash-poor economy.

But this was not all. By seizing California the South would gain a vast area and extend slavery clear to the Pacific coast. Aside from the international prestige thus gained, the South could then prepare a formidable base for building up a flank attack against the Union. At the same time, the existence of such a base would be very suitable for annexing much of the Far West, the Southwest and a sizable portion of northern Mexico.

In fact, the mastery of California, if achieved by the expansion-minded South, might conceivably have tipped the balance of the war in the South's favor—or at least allowed it to put up an even tougher resistance than it did.

101

On the face of it, though, it seemed that California was certain to take sides with the North; after all, it had been admitted as a "free" state—slavery was forbidden within its borders. Actually, the matter was not so simple, for many of its citizens—perhaps half—were of southern extraction and favored the southern cause.

Likewise, some rich people who wanted to side with the likely winner favored the South because it scored most of the early military victories of the war. Much of the Spanish and Mexican population sided with the South because of the assurances given it that the Confederacy would validate dubious land titles.

Similarly, squatters and trespassers who had reason to fear the actions of legally constituted government favored the South because they had been assured that their unjustified land claims would be legalized by a victorious Confederacy.

Finally, a substantial portion of California's population was indifferent about the outcome of the war, which consequently weakened support for the Union.

Even Senator Gwin, who had been so interested in the plan for obtaining a government mail contract for Russell, Majors & Waddell, turned against the Union. Being of southern birth he naturally sympathized with the Confederacy and joined it on the outbreak of war.

In December, 1859, Gwin delivered a speech in the Senate in which he stated that "All slave-holding states of this Confederacy can establish a separate and independent government that will be impregnable to the assaults of all foreign enemies." He went on to say that if the southern states seceded, "California would be with them." Though he subsequently had these remarks stricken from the record, wind of them came to California and served to discredit him.

After the South was defeated, Gwin fled to Mexico

where the Emperor Maximilian made him Duke of the Province of Sonora. When Maximilian was defeated and executed, Gwin returned to California, where he lived out his remaining years in uneventful retirement. He never lived down the derisive nickname of "Duke."

California also had a "neutralist" group, made up mainly of northerners, who took the position that in the event of civil war California should stand aside from the conflict and form an independent country. This separatist sentiment was naturally fostered by California's remoteness from the rest of the country. We might note in passing that the Pony Express, by linking California with the other states, was helping to keep California loyal to the Union.

One of the most prominent exponents of the separatist idea, a former New Englander named F. A. Buck, came out for Californian independence in this forthright though hardly patriotic statement:

> We shall secede, with the Rocky Mountains for a line, and form an Empire of the Pacific, with Washington Territory, Oregon, and California, and we shall annex all of this side of Mexico. We don't care a straw whether you dissolve the Union or not. We just wish that the Republicans and the Democrats at the Capitol would get into a fight and kill each other off like the Kilkenny cats. Perhaps that would settle the hash.

Interestingly enough, once the war did come, Mr. Buck quickly changed his mind and became one of the most fervent backers of the Union side!

But the northern cause had its supporters too. Foremost among these was the press, which had a strong sense of loyalty to the Union. The press appealed not only to patriotic sentiment but also to motives of self-interest. It pointed out that the prospect of a transcontinental railroad would go glimmering if California went over to the Confederate side.

Abraham Lincoln was elected President on November 7, 1860. As soon as the electrifying news reached St. Joseph by telegraph, a Pony Express rider set out on the first leg of the long journey to Fort Churchill, Nevada, which was now linked by telegraph with San Francisco. The Pony Express was still needed to cover the eighteen hundred miles between St. Joseph and Fort Churchill. Thanks to its services, San Francisco papers were able to carry the news of Lincoln's election in their editions of November 19.

Lincoln's victory heartened the Union forces in California. Swiftly the state legislature passed a resolution pledging its support to the Union. Again the Pony Express proved its value by speeding this welcome news eastward. Meanwhile it was bringing specially prepared copies of eastern newspapers printed on lightweight paper to save postage. This service enabled Californians to keep in close touch with the rest of the country as the move toward war gained impetus.

As 1860 drew to a close a serious situation developed in California. A group of southern sympathizers, known as the Knights of the Golden Circle, was organized with a view to seizing the Mexican state of Sonora, forming an independent Republic of the Pacific, and then joining the Confederacy after the southern states seceded from the Union.

The basic military idea was to seize the Presidio at the entrance to the Golden Gate, as well as the forts on

Alcatraz Island, the Customs House, the Mint, the Post Office and all other government property.

John B. Floyd, who was President Buchanan's Secretary of War, gave up his post to fight for the Confederacy. According to H. H. Bancroft, the famous historian, Floyd, during his term of office, ordered the removal of 135,000 firearms and revolvers, as well as a large quantity of ammunition and cannon, from the government arsenal at Springfield, Mass. to various arsenals in the South and Southwest. It is said that fifty thousand muskets were shipped to California as part of this shifting process. At no time did Floyd reveal to Congress what he was doing.

With sixteen thousand members, the conspiratorial group could not very well keep its plans secret; soon it became common knowledge that the conspirators were receiving fifty thousand muskets from Springfield.

The Pony Express brought back the news of the conspiracy to Missouri, from where it was telegraphed to Washington. In turn, Washington sent instructions for putting down the insurrection before it could properly get under way. These instructions were of course brought to California by the Pony Express. In the transmission of these messages the government relied almost completely on the Pony Express. There was a significant reason for this. Previously, as we know, Washington had favored the Butterfield Route, which was longer and much slower. This choice had been dictated by southern members of Congress. But now the federal government could no longer resort to the Butterfield Route, which was mostly staffed by men sympathetic to the southern cause.

The Butterfield Route was of course the "chosen instrument" of the southerners. However, since it was ten days slower than the Pony Express route, the federal government enjoyed a distinct advantage in its communications with California.

But meanwhile the Pony Express was in dire need of money. A bill was presented in Congress to make the Central Overland Route the official mail route, with the Pony Express carrying two mails in each direction every week, and with a million-dollar subsidy to be paid the Pony Express by the Post Office Department every year.

President Buchanan, who was slated to remain President until March 4, 1861, gave the bill no support. The bill died in Congress with no action taken. Valiantly, the Pony Express carried on, although its days were now surely numbered. Eagerly the people of the West waited for the new President's message.

As the inaugural date of March 4, 1861, drew near, the Pony Express was put in readiness to carry Lincoln's inaugural address to California. The line was alerted from St. Joseph to Sacramento—nothing was to interfere with this urgent business. Extra horses and extra riders were placed strategically along the route.

It took three days for the text of the address to arrive at St. Joseph by train. From there the Express couriers took over and set an amazing pace; two of the riders, in their eagerness to make up for delays, actually rode their horses to death. The carrying of the inaugural address established the all-time Pony Express record: St. Joseph to Sacramento in seven days and seventeen hours.

On March 17, less than two weeks after the President's inauguration, Lincoln's address was published in the San Francisco newspapers. California was astounded at this rapid transmission of the news. The new President's message of confidence and his resolute insistence on keeping the Union intact revived the drooping spirits of Union sympathizers in California.

The state legislature likewise remained loyal to the Union, passing a resolution in the winter of 1860–61 which stated that "California is ready to maintain the rights and honor of the National Government at home and abroad, and at all times to respond to any requisitions that may be made upon her to defend the Republic against foreign or domestic foes." This forthright resolution helped to heighten the morale of Californians who stood on the side of the Union.

Early in 1861, General Albert Sidney Johnston, head of the Military Department of the Pacific, resigned to fight for the Confederacy. The War Department replaced Johnston with General Edwin A. Sumner, an energetic and able officer.

General Sumner immediately took decisive action. First he posted a detachment of soldiers near Los Angeles to put down any revolt that might break out. Confederate sympathizers moved to Nevada, where they made common cause with like-minded people. On June 5, 1861, they raised the Confederate flag at Virginia City in Nevada.

General Sumner lost no time in quelling the uprising. He sent a force to Nevada which disarmed and dispersed a rebel militia company. Fort Churchill was strengthened to prevent any further outbreak. With the revolt nipped in the bud, General Sumner had taken an important step forward in protecting California from the contagion of revolt.

While taking these measures General Sumner raised

and drilled additional troops to cope with any further uprisings. Throughout this trying time Sumner kept in constant touch with Washington. Here the Pony Express played a vital role in speeding communications between California and the nation's capital. It may well be that without the speedy delivery of important messages there would have been a serious danger of California's being lost to the Union.

Late in 1862, General Sumner was called back to duty in the East. His replacement, Colonel George Wright, was another very able man who devoted all his efforts to keeping California in the Union column. There were other important tasks—patrol duties to prevent Indian revolts, garrisoning forts, protecting the mail routes and guarding the frontier. During this trying time California raised more troops than the Union had possessed at the outbreak of the Civil War. During the most critical time, 1860–61, the Pony Express made a contribution that was deeply appreciated by California patriots. Bancroft eloquently expressed this feeling:

> It was the pony to which everyone looked for deliverance; men prayed for the safety of the little beast, and trembled lest the service should be discontinued. Great was the relief of the people when Hole's bill for a daily mail service was passed and the service changed from the Southern to the Central route, as it was early in the summer [of 1861]. Yet after all, it was to the flying pony that all eyes and hearts were turned.

10   *Dark Days for the Pony Express*

As the Civil War got under way, the volume of freighting business handled by Russell's firm began to fall off very sharply. In anticipation of the coming struggle, the War Department had already started to shift troops from the western posts to the East. Fewer supplies were needed at these posts and this was clearly reflected in freight shipments.

With operations steadily becoming more unprofitable, there was a distinct likelihood that the Pony Express would be dropped. Westerners were alarmed—and thoroughly angry at this prospect, as the following blunt editorial in the *Sacramento Union* makes clear:

> There is a strong possibility that the Pony Express will be discontinued. Our correspondent in St. Louis says it is pretty well settled that Russell & Co. will get no mail contract, and, as the Pony Express is now a total loss, almost, to them, there is no inducement to continue it.
>
> Our correspondent adds that the people may thank Postmaster General Holt and our plotting Senator, Gwin, for it. The former is about 100 years behind the age and should go home and cultivate a tobacco plantation. The latter should be expelled from California just as soon as the

votes of the people, through the Legislature, can be brought to bear upon his Senatorial aspirations.

The concluding part of this comment is a clear indication that Gwin's pro-southern sympathies were no secret—if they ever had been.

The name of the Central Overland California & Pike's Peak Express Company had been put together with a grandiloquent optimism that reflected Russell's high hopes. It had sunk to such a low estate that it was nicknamed "Clean Out of Cash & Poor Pay."

By the beginning of 1861, the firm's creditors were so worried that they tried to get their hands on some of the organization's property. In February, the *Deseret News* expressed the fears of the people of Salt Lake about this threat:

> A few days since, there was a little excitement raised in this city, by the circulation of a report that all the stock belonging to the Mail and Express Company in this Territory, had been attached at the suit of Livingston, Bell & Co.; in consequence of which the Mail and Express would be stopped, and no further communications might be expected from the east very soon; which, in these very exciting times would certainly be a great inconvenience, not to say calamity.

Later on, the paper saw a silver lining: even if the firm's property was taken over, the Pony Express would be continued—possibly on a sounder financial basis:

> The report that the animals had been attached was

correct, but we are credibly informed that there was no intention on the part of the plaintiffs in the case to interfere with the transmission of the mail, nor to prevent the "pony" from making its regular trips, for the present at least; and not at all, if the matter of indebtedness shall be otherwise satisfactorily adjusted. If we rightly understand the matter, the transaction may be considered more favorable than otherwise to the continuance of the existing mail and express arrangements.

Still, the last melancholy phase of the Pony Express had started. The Butterfield Route was not much better off. It was run so badly that the cost of carrying a letter skyrocketed to almost seventy dollars. Though it was certain that the South would seize the route as soon as civil war erupted, the government still continued to pay the monstrous costs of operating the Butterfield Route.

Finally Congress acted. The Butterfield contract was transferred to the Central Route, along with coaches, stock, and equipment. The company then joined operations with Russell, Majors & Waddell, who shared the annual million-dollar subsidy: $475,000 to Russell, Majors & Waddell, and $525,000 to the Overland Mail Company. The two companies continued to operate as separate corporations.

According to the contract, the two companies were to rely on stagecoaches to carry the mails. They were to operate six schedules a week and to cover at least 112 miles a day—about half the mileage made by Pony Express riders.

Still the Pony Express continued to perform its job

faithfully and efficiently. When the Civil War began with the Confederates firing on Fort Sumter on March 12, 1861, it was the Pony Express that brought the devastating news to California.

Meanwhile, the financial problems of the Pony Express continued to mount. The Express was carrying the mail at an average loss of thirteen dollars per letter. Obviously, this state of affairs could not go on much longer. How then, did the organization remain in business? At this critical point this interesting question received a spectacular answer as the Pony Express was rocked by an unsavory scandal which made front-page headlines all over the country.

A clerk named Godard Bailey, employed by the Department of the Interior, had withdrawn $870,000 worth of Indian Affairs bonds held in trust with that department and had turned them over to Mr. Russell. The disappearance of the bonds was announced on December 24, 1860, and on the same day Russell was arrested and held for $200,000 bail. Friends immediately offered more than two million dollars for bail, and Russell was soon released.

Some of the tangled details of this involved affair have not been unraveled to this day. But in general outline this seems to have been the sequence. By early 1858, the Department of the Interior owed Russell's freighting firm about $500,000 which it could not pay because it did not have the funds. Russell proposed to John B. Floyd, the Secretary of War, that his department issue acceptances. These were documents acknowledging the existence of the debt and promising to pay it at a later date.

Russell in turn promised not to present these acceptances for payment on their due date. Instead he agreed to put them up for security with New York bankers for a loan.

Between March 25, 1858, and October 1, 1860, Floyd issued over five million dollars worth of these acceptances to various firms. Russell's firm held about $861,000 worth of these acceptances.

Somewhere between October 1, 1860, and December 24, Godard Bailey took $870,000 worth of Indian Affairs bonds from a department safe. Why?

It seems a plausible guess that when Russell tried to use the acceptances he had received for security for loans, the New York bankers refused to take the acceptances, since they were not permitted to be presented for payment on their due dates. In effect, they must have said to Russell: "If you want to borrow money from us, you'll have to give us better security."

So here was Russell, cruelly strapped for money and unable to collect on the debt owed him by the government. He must have gone back to the government officials and explained his dilemma.

The Secretaries of the Interior and War had to do something to get Russell out of his predicament. The solution, apparently, was to make the government bonds available to Russell so that he could use them for collateral to get a loan. Presumably, Bailey acted as a go-between on orders from his superiors. He gave Russell $870,000 worth of the abstracted Indian Affairs bonds and received the acceptances of a like amount as security for the bonds.

All this was done in secrecy, of course, so the people involved clearly knew they were doing something wrong. As far as Russell was concerned, he does not seem to have had any consciousness of guilt. His intention was doubtless to pay off his loan, get back the bonds and return them to the government. Thus he would have been released from his most stringent financial difficulties, while the government would have back its bonds.

Though Russell's intentions may have been of the best, his methods were inexcusable. When the scandal broke, he had to dig heavily into his private fortune and borrow a considerable sum from Ben Holladay, a stagecoach magnate. Russell always stoutly maintained his innocence. His word was accepted in the West. When he returned to the western scene he was given a testimonial ball attended by many notable people, including governors of states and territories.

Secretary of War Floyd's version of what had happened was summarized in this way by the *New York Herald*:

> Floyd had allowed Russell to draw upon his department for $100,000. This had been repeated six or seven times, Floyd's friends saying that each time he thought that Russell was merely renewing and not accumulating the drafts.
>
> A friend approached Bailey (who was said to be married to a niece of Floyd) and told him that his uncle would be ruined and that Bailey could save him by allowing him to use the state stocks held in trust for the Indians as against the acceptances given to Russell.

The Congressional investigation which followed, however, showed that Floyd had by no means been so innocent. The disillusioned *Herald* printed headlines like this one:

JOHN B. FLOYD, LATE SECRETARY OF WAR,
CAPTAIN OF THE FORTY THIEVES

By this time Floyd was safely back in Virginia, working for the Confederacy and against the government in which he had recently held one of the top positions of trust.

The committee report was unsparing in its criticism of Floyd, whom it called "a bankrupt in fortune and a political adventurer." Further, the committee pointed out that Floyd had issued acceptances to others, and that the practice had been forbidden by President Buchanan.

Nor, it must be confessed, did Russell come off much better. The committee characterized his testimony as "vague, rambling and unsatisfactory," adding that "He shows such utter ignorance of the details of his business, or unwillingness to make an exhibit of his affairs that your committee have considered it much safer to base their conclusions on the records furnished by the War Department."

The historian H. H. Bancroft hinted that Russell became involved in the bond fraud as part of an intrigue intended to discredit him and deprive him of the opportunity to get government help. This is what Bancroft had to say on the subject:

In January, 1861, Russell, president of the company, fell into difficulty—if, indeed, it were not a trap set for him by friends of the southern route. The company was largely in debt, owing about $1,800,-000; and, although a large company, and with considerable assets, was embarrassed to a degree which made borrowing necessary to a greater extent than was convenient. The government was also in debt to the company on its contracts, Congress having failed to pass an appropriation bill.

While Russell was in Washington, endeavoring to secure some relief, he was induced to take $870,000 in bonds of the Interior Department, as a loan, and given as security acceptances of the War Department, furnished him by Secretary Floyd, a part of which was not yet due. The bonds, as it turned out, were stolen by Godard Bailey, a family connection of Floyd's, and law clerk in the Interior Department. In the temporary confusion which followed the discovery of the fraud, Russell lost his opportunity, as perhaps it was meant that he should.

Congress in February, 1861, authorized the Postmaster General to advertise for bids for a daily mail service over the central route.

Russell never claimed that he had been duped by anybody. He defended his taking of the bonds on the ground that the government owed his firm a huge sum that he was entitled to recoup.

As for Secretary of the Interior Jacob Thompson, he resigned in January, 1861. In his *History of the Southern Rebellion,* Orville J. Victor gives this summary of Thompson's subsequent career:

He was appointed aide to General Beauregard. From 1862 to 1864 Thompson was Governor of Mississippi. After the assassination of Lincoln, Thompson was accused of complicity, and a price was put on his head. He then escaped to Europe.

When he returned he was brought to trial and a civil suit was brought in 1876 for the money taken by Bailey while Thompson was Secretary of the Interior.

The fact that Gwin, Floyd and Thompson were all strong supporters of the Confederacy lends some color to the speculation that they took part in varying degrees in an intrigue to deprive the North of the mail routes by discrediting Russell. Nevertheless, this must remain in the realm of speculation.

On the other hand, if Russell was a dupe, he was a willing dupe, rendered desperate, no doubt, by his pressing financial difficulties. It is hard to believe that in the matter of the bonds he emerged with completely clean hands. A sorry story, in painful contrast to the heroism and devotion of the Pony Express riders.

Regardless of what underlying facts were involved in this scandal, the fate of the Pony Express was now sealed. The company would never be able to get a mail contract from the government.

The man to whom Butterfield sold out, Benjamin Holladay, was a colorful Kentuckian. Holladay had had a variety of careers: he had been a mule skinner and cowboy, and had finally struck it rich as part owner of a highly productive mine. Holladay was an experienced stage line operator who knew the business well. He was also on very friendly terms with the owners of the Pony Express.

It was in his dress that Holladay let his flamboyant imagination run riot. All the buttons on his waistcoat, for example, were jewels—each one different. He topped this off with a fabulously expensive emerald scarf pin. When he crossed the route line from St.

Joseph to Sacramento in his famous coach, he was given a royal welcome wherever he appeared. Brass bands blared and cannon thundered in his honor. Welcoming speeches and flattering newspaper articles followed with monotonous regularity.

In one of these articles he was called the Emperor of Transportation—very appropriately, for his tastes and manners were surely imperial. When a Denver newspaper complained that Holladay's rates were exorbitant, he did not deign to make a reply. Instead, he modified the route so that it now veered sixty miles away from Denver.

Under Holladay the Central Overland Mail prospered. In its palmiest days it had more than a hundred stagecoaches and almost two thousand animals. Eventually Holladay sold out for two million dollars. (The original management had run the Pony Express for eighteen months at a loss of $500,000. But with a million-dollar mail contract this would have been changed into a $500,000 profit.)

Although the bulk of the mail was now carried by stagecoaches, the Pony Express continued to be used for fast mail. All newspaper stories on the war were carried by the Pony Express from Fort Kearny to Fort Churchill. Similarly, important news from California traveled the same route eastward.

On October 24, 1861, the transcontinental telegraph was completed, and its magnetic click replaced the melodious hoofbeats of the ponies. On March 7, 1862, several months after the close of the Pony Express, Holladay took over the company and its stage line operations and mail contracts. His magnificent coach was drawn by eight horses, and was richly furnished and decorated. It had, among other unusual features, silk curtains and silver candlesticks.

Meanwhile, Holladay continued to pile up wealth. He had an ornate mansion in New York, an equally sumptuous one in Washington, and a beautiful estate in Westchester County in New York state. During his trips over the Overland Mail Route, he was known to have paid for a breakfast of corn bread and bacon with a twenty dollar gold piece. But he never lost the common touch. There is a story—doubtless untrue but quite in character—that his famous coach was once stopped by highwaymen. While one of the robbers pawed over his luggage for loot, another held Holladay at bay with a Colt revolver. Finding it irksome to keep his hands up, Holladay said to his guard, "My nose itches. May I scratch it?"

"Don't bother," the bandit replied. "I'll scratch it for you"—and he did, with the muzzle of his pistol.

Originally there were eighty Pony Express riders, but because of the privations and dangers of the job, many resigned. As a result, the total number of riders never amounted to more than 120. These 120 riders rode 650,000 miles—yet only one rider was killed by the Indians, only one relatively unimportant pack of mail was lost, and only one schedule failed to be completed.

The Pony Express was finally brought to an end, not by the stagecoaches, but by the completion of the transcontinental telegraph.

But before we see how this came to pass, it might be interesting to get a glimpse into the future of the three men whose names are most closely linked with the Pony Express.

Russell became a forgotten man. Bankers and financiers shunned him. During his last years he lived at the house of his son and died in 1872.

Waddell never went back into business. His later life was full of misfortune. One of his sons was killed in the Civil War. His home was raided repeatedly by Union soldiers until he submitted to the indignity of signing an oath of loyalty to the United States.

But this was not all. He was harried by lawsuits; some of his property was sold off to pay taxes; his friends turned against him. He died at the home of his daughter in 1872, a few months before Russell's death.

Majors, made of sterner stuff, remained in the freighting business. In 1867, he moved to Salt Lake City and took part in the construction of the Union Pacific Railroad. Subsequently, he participated in several unsuccessful business ventures. He died in 1900.

And Big Ben Holladay? He lost most of his fortune in the Panic of 1873, had to sell his luxurious mansions and his beautiful estate, and died a comparatively poor man.

Thus, a tragic destiny seemed to pursue these men, leaving them ultimately with little more than memories of their former power and wealth.

These were the men who had done more than any others to open up the Central Route to the Pacific in those explosive years between the Mexican and Civil Wars.

Russell, Majors & Waddell had put on the first Wild West Show with the Pony Express. Everyone applauded —but no one paid at the gate.

11 *The Telegraph Replaces the Pony Express*

WE HAVE SEEN that despite its financial failure the Pony Express did succeed in achieving its objective of delivering mail between Missouri and California in ten days. Thus, California became a real part of the Union despite the intervening distance of two thousand miles.

But even at the very time the Pony Express started, its days were numbered. For everyone knew that sooner or later the telegraph lines would be extended all the way to the coast. Then the dots and dashes would at last provide instantaneous communication.

In fact, it took only eight months after the greatest feat of the Pony Express—the delivery of the text of Lincoln's First Inaugural—for the telegraph lines to be put up all the way across the continent. In 1857, Hiram Sibley, president of Western Union, suggested to his board of directors that it was time to extend the telegraph lines to California. While the directors were not opposed, they prudently proposed that the construction be done by a company made up of all the existing telegraph firms. But when Sibley called such a meeting to propose transcontinental telegraph communication, his colleagues merely laughed at him for his impractical and visionary ideas.

Think of the huge expense involved, they pointed out. And what about the Indians? And the tremendous maintenance costs—especially in wintertime? Very well,

Sibley replied: Western Union will do the job by itself. After drawing up his plans he went to Washington and tried to interest Congress in the project.

The legislators were more interested in the transcontinental telegraph than they had been in the Pony Express. Doubtless the desperate character of the threatening civil war had brought home to them the urgent need for better communications. They passed a bill providing for a $40,000 loan a year for ten years, the total to be repaid by Western Union after completion of the line.

Sibley then went ahead without ever borrowing any of the funds provided. When the Civil War broke out, he became more determined than ever to build the line. After forming the Postal Telegraph Company for this purpose, he set up two competing construction companies.

One of these, under Edward Creighton, worked west from Omaha in Nebraska. The other, under James Gamble, worked east from Fort Churchill in Nevada. A handsome prize was to be awarded to the party that first reached Salt Lake City.

Actually the group working west from Omaha had more ground to cover on the plains and over the Rockies. But the other group working eastward had to traverse the Great American Desert, and considering the difficulty of this forbidding terrain, the race was a fair one.

Both groups were able to make steady progress because they wisely divided up the work in small groups. One group, using twenty-six wagons drawn by oxen, distributed poles, wires, and all other necessary mate-

Election news.

Lincoln elected—

Benham Esq

Styles Bros

for the Rocky Mountain News

to Denver.

PONY EXPRESS
NOV 8
ST. JOSEPH.

THE CENTRAL OVERLAND CALIFORNIA
& PIKES PEAK
EXPRESS COMPANY
NOV 8
ST. JOSEPH. MO.

PONY EXPRESS HISTORY AND ART GALLERY

News of Lincoln's election is carried west by Pony Express.

The transcontinental telegraph replaces the Pony Express.

rials along the trail. Another group laid out the line and drove stakes to indicate the location of the poles. Others dug the holes, followed by a group that set up the poles. There were two other groups: one strung the wires between the poles, while the other did the cooking, and set up a camp each afternoon, and broke it up the following morning.

At first, the Indians were hostile, or at least bewildered by this strange construction. However, Creighton explained to them that the device was a gift from the Great Spirit to make it possible to carry a man's voice hundreds of miles. The Indians remained skeptical, but they came round when Creighton asked Chief Washakie of the Shoshones to send a message to another chief in far-off Wyoming, arranging for a meeting at a mid point at a given time. When both Indians showed up at the rendezvous on scheduled time, they were finally convinced.

As the construction parties advanced they built stations on the way. As fast as the stations were built they were manned by competent telegraphers. The work went on so smoothly that by the summer of 1861, the Pony Express riders were limited to runs of only a few hundred miles.

It took Gamble a whole month to get his equipment wagons and workers across the Sierra Nevada Mountains to Carson City in Nevada. As there was surprisingly heavy traffic on the roads, it was late June by the time the lumbering wagons rolled into Carson City.

Once a hole was dug, a crew of four or five workmen set the pole in place. Where the soil was loose and dry it was necessary to support the base with piles of rocks.

At this point a new working crew arrived in wagons loaded with ladders and large reels of wire. They strung the wire from pole to pole, completing the job.

In October, Gamble ran into trouble. At a point when he was nearly finished with his work he ran out of poles. He tried to hire men to cut down trees, but they were afraid they might be trapped by a blizzard. A stoppage at this stage would very likely delay the completion of the work to the following spring. Finally, he managed to persuade a group to undertake the cutting, on condition that he stayed with them and shared the risk. The cutting was finished in a few days, and the completion of the whole job took place in a very short time.

On October 22, 1861, Gamble's team won the race when they reached Salt Lake City, connecting that city with the Pacific coast by telegraph. Creighton's team arrived in Salt Lake only two days later. At last, the United States had its first transcontinental telegraph system: Washington was able to communicate directly with San Francisco over a distance of three thousand miles.

Stephen J. Field, Chief Justice of California, commemorated the completion of the line by telegraphing the following message to President Lincoln:

In the temporary absence of the Governor of the State, I am requested to send you the first message which will be transmitted over the wires of the telegraph line which connects the Pacific with the Atlantic states. The people of California desire to congratulate you upon the completion of this great work. They believe that it will be the means of strengthening the attachment which binds both the East and West to the Union, and they desire in this— the first message across the continent—to express their loyalty to the Union and their determination to stand by its Government on this its day of trial. They regard that Government with affection and will adhere to it under all fortunes.

The transcontinental telegraph had effectively completed the work of the Pony Express in connecting far-off California with the rest of the Union.

The Pony Express was officially discontinued on October 26, 1861, though it actually ran for several more weeks. Important messages were switched to the telegraph. The last Pony Express mail was delivered in November. The equipment and animals were sold, the stations abandoned.

Though the Pony Express had operated for a mere eighteen months, it was more than a business; it was a romantic adventure which thrilled the people of its own day and those of later times as well.

The western press was full of heartfelt tributes to the Pony Express. Here is a representative one from the *Pacific*:

A fast and faithful friend has the Pony been to our far-off state. Summer and winter, storm and shine, day and night, he has traveled like a weaver's shuttle back and forth till now his work is done. Good-bye, Pony! No proud and star-caparisoned charger in the war field has ever done so great, so true and so good a work as thine. No pampered and world-famed racer of the turf will ever win from you the proud fame of the fleet courser of the continent.

You came to us often with tidings that made your feet beautiful on the tops of the mountains; tidings of the world's great life, of nations rising for liberty and winning the day of battles, and nations' defeats and reverses. We have looked for you as those who wait for the morning, and how seldom did you fail us! When days were months and hours weeks, how you thrilled us out of our pain and suspense, to know the best or know the worst! You have served us well!

An even more moving tribute came from the *Sacramento Bee*:

Farewell, Pony: Farewell and forever, thou staunch, wilderness-overcoming, swift-footed messenger. Thou wert the pioneer of the continent in the rapid transmission of intelligence between its peoples, and have dragged in your train the lightning itself, which, in good time, will be followed by steam communication by rail. Rest upon your honors; be satisfied with them, your destiny has been fulfilled—a new and higher power has superseded you.

This is no disgrace, for flesh and blood cannot always war against the elements. Rest, then, in peace; for thou hast run thy race, thou hast followed thy course, thou hast done the work that was given thee to do.

The Pony Express helped to preserve California for the Union. It brought the news of great battles to the Far West. Newspaper editors depended on it for the latest news. Merchants arranged important deals by the use of the Pony Express.

A whole nation was enthralled by the quiet heroism

and magnificent endurance of the Pony Express riders. They created an epic in the winning of the West which will be remembered as long as the spirit of adventure remains alive in American hearts and minds.